101
Quick Strike
Inbound Plays

Bruce Eamon Brown

ISBN: 1-58518-872-7
Library of Congress Control Number: 2003111049
Cover design: Kerry Hartjen
Text design and diagrams: Jeanne Hamilton
Front cover photo: Craig Jones/Getty Images

Coaches Choice
P.O. Box 1828
Monterey, CA 93942
www.coacheschoice.com

Dedication

To all coaches whose teaching style promotes fearless play in their athletes.

Preface

Keep it *simple* and think *attack*! Inbound plays should not require a lot of teaching time, yet they are excellent opportunities to place the defense in immediate and difficult situations. With a few exceptions, every inbound play should be designed to score. Inbound plays do not need to be complex to be effective. It is much better to have simple, quick attacking plays designed to get the ball in the hands of the right players on the right place on the floor. If an inbound play requires more than two diagrams to explain the movement, it is probably too much for your players to think about. Keep in mind that you get to place your players in any positions you want prior to the play starting, the ball is only about 6 to 10 feet from the basket, and the passer is basically unguarded since he gets three feet of space to inbound the ball. Get your offensive cutters moving aggressively and quickly toward the basket, coming off screens that provide an advantage in space or physical mismatches. Get the ball in the hands of shooters or post players where they are the most effective. Choose plays with offensive moves and screens that are difficult to defend at your age level. Think *attack*!

The plays in this book represent a variety of options. They are all quick strike plays designed to get a shot in one to three passes. None of the plays develop slowly or take much time to get your team into position to score. Identify three or four inbound plays that fit your system, age, and ability level, and then execute them consistently and perfectly.

As you read through the drills, realize that each play is described and illustrated from the same side of the floor. This is only for convenience and ease of understanding. You must practice them from both sides of the court. Also, in most plays, the number 1 is used as the player inbounding the ball. You may want to have a taller player inbound the ball. In the diagrams, a player other than 1 is shown inbounding the ball only when there was a special need. The player inbounding the ball must have good vision and poise. Instead of using terms such as power forward and strong guard, this book numbers the players from 1 to 5. The numbers can mean whatever fits your personnel. Keep in mind that each age level has a different perspective on what a "center" may be. At your level, a "center" may be 5'8" or 6'8". In general, 1 is usually the best ballhandling guard, 2 and 3 are normally more active players with perimeter shooting ability, and 4 and 5 are usually larger, interior players. Look at the whole play and then place your players where it is most advantageous for their skills, instead of strictly placing them according to the numbers in this book. Decide which players you want setting screens, receiving screens, shooting perimeter shots, posting up, and receiving lob passes, and then place them there.

Many coaches are just concerned with getting the ball inbounds safely and then setting up their offense. You may never have a better chance to score than when you have the ball out-of-bounds. Don't be conservative—*attack* the basket with inbound plays designed to score.

Contents

Diagram Key

Offensive Players = 1, 2, 3, 4, 5

Offensive Player with the Ball = ①

Defensive Player = **X**

Pass = **2- - - - - - ➛ 3**

Cut or Path of a Player = **4** ⌒⬎

Dribbler = ①〰➚

Screen = **5 ———⊣**

Example
Offensive player with the ball (1) passes to 2 and then cuts
and sets a screen on 3.

Court Diagram

In the sample diagram, 1 has the ball.

Block = The mark on the side of the key at the low post
    4 is on the *ballside block*
    5 is on the *opposite block* (away from the ball)

Elbow = The corner at the end of the foul line and the key
    2 is on the *ballside elbow*
    3 is on the *opposite elbow* (away from the ball)

Wing = Area near the three-point line and the foul line extended
    A represents the *ballside wing*
    B represents the *opposite wing*

Corner = Area near the three-point line directly out from the block
    C represents the *ballside corner*
    D represents the *opposite corner*

Short Corner or Feeder Spot = Area about six feet off the key and near the baseline
    E represents the *ballside feeder spot*
    F represents the *opposite feeder spot*

1

Box Sets

PLAY #1: BOX SET VERSUS A MAN-TO-MAN DEFENSE

Objective: Double-screen for shooter and post slip.

Description: From a box set, 5 lines up on the opposite block, 4 on the opposite elbow, 3 on the ballside block, and 2 at the ballside elbow. 3 starts by clearing to the far corner and spotting up on the three-point line. 4 screens across for the best shooter (2). 2 V-cuts to receive 4's screen and continues on, curling off 5's screen toward the basket. After screening, 4 slips the screen and cuts directly toward the ball. 5 sets the second screen for 2, delays to read the other cutters, and then can release to the perimeter to be the safe outlet.

Coaching Points:

- 1 reads, sequentially, 3, 4, 2 for a shot, and then 5 as a safe inbounds pass.

- 3 and 4 make their cuts quickly and target the ball with their hands.

- 2 sets up his cut off 4 and then rubs shoulder to shoulder with 5 reading whether to curl or fade.

- Sequential passing reads are 4, 2, 5.

- All players need to be ready to reposition themselves to become safety outlets.

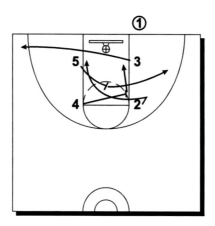

PLAY #2: BOX SET VERSUS A MAN-TO-MAN DEFENSE

Objective: Move three cutters toward the ball. Double-screen for best shooter (2). Screen the screener, and roll off the screen.

Description: From a box set, 5 starts on the opposite block, 4 on the opposite elbow, 3 on the ballside block, and 2 on the ballside elbow. 2 V-cuts to set up the screen from 4 and continues to receive screen from 5. He reads curl or fade. 4 sets a cross screen for 2 and then receives a back screen from 3 and cuts to the basket. 3 steps, delays slightly, sets a back screen for 4, and then rolls toward the basket. 5 sets the second screen for 2 and then delays to read the other cutters and can release to the perimeter to become the safe outlet.

Coaching Points:

- The better the screen that 4 sets, the more likely his defender will have to help and the more open either 4 or 3 will be on their cuts to the basket.

- 3 delays slightly and can step in to try to pin his defender before setting the back screen on 4's defender.

- 2 rubs tightly off both screens and reads the defender on whether to curl to the basket or fade to the perimeter.

- Sequential passing reads are 4, 3, 2, and then 5 for the safe outlet.

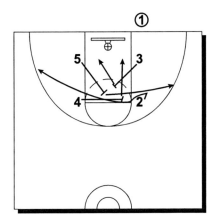

PLAY #3: BOX SET VERSUS A MAN-TO-MAN DEFENSE

Objective: Down screens for the shooters, post-ups for the big players, and then a screen for the inbounder.

Description: From a box set, 3 starts on the opposite block, 5 at the opposite elbow, 2 on the ballside block, and 4 on the ballside elbow. 2 cuts up toward a stationary 4 and then curls out to the wing on the side of the ball. 5 sets a down screen for 3. 3 curls toward the ballside of the floor. After screening, 5 rolls and attempts to post up his defender. After 2 curls off 4, 4 screens down for 1. 1 inbounds the ball and then delays slightly before cutting off the screen set by 4, looking for a short jumper or post feed.

Coaching Points:

- 2 can look like he is going to set a pick for 4 before curling off 4 to the outside.

- If 2's defender starts cheating to the outside of the screen, 2 can break the pattern and cut back to the basket.

- The same play can be run if the inbound pass goes to 3.

- Sequential passing reads are 2, 4, 3, and then 5 as the safety outlet.

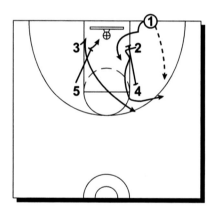

PLAY #4: BOX SET VERSUS A MAN-TO-MAN DEFENSE

Objective: Allow post to operate with a clear side of the floor and get either the initial pass or a high-low feed from 5.

Description: From a box set, 5 starts on the opposite block, 4 on the opposite elbow, 2 on the ballside block, and 3 on the ballside elbow. 2 and 3 clear to the side opposite the inbounder. 4 screens for 3, then steps out to receive a screen from 5 and curl back to the basket. The pass can be a lob or a direct pass if 4 beats his defender across the key. If the defender is between the ball and 4 on the cut, the inbound pass should go to 5 at the high post. 5 then looks to make a high-low pass to 4, who seals the defender on the baseline side. After passing, 1 should cut opposite the pass.

Coaching Points:

- 3 cuts hard off of 4's screen and calls for the ball on the three-point line.

- As 4 cuts off 5's screen, he must work to keep the defender on one side or the other.

- If the defender trails 4, then 4 must attempt to keep the defender on his back to get the direct pass from 1.

- If the defender beats 4 to the ball, then 4 must attempt to spin and seal the defender on the baseline side and anticipate the pass to be entered to 5, who will make an immediate high-low pass to 4.

- Sequential passing reads are 4, 5, then 2 or 3 as safety outlets.

PLAY #5: BOX SET VERSUS A MAN-TO-MAN DEFENSE

Objective: Shooters circle to the perimeter and the two posts cut toward the basket.

Description: From the box set, 3 starts on the opposite block, 2 on the opposite elbow, 4 on the ballside block, and 5 on the ballside elbow. 2 initiates the play and cuts low to the ballside corner, and 3 cuts off of 5 to the ballside wing and spots up for a shot. 4 moves up the lane and as 3 cuts off of 5, 4 curls back to the openside of the key, over the top of 5. After screening for cutters (3 and 4), 5 slips directly back to the ball, looking for a direct pass. If a safety pass is required, 4 can step to the ballside corner.

Coaching Points:

*   2 and 3 need to cut quickly and hard.

*   As 4 moves up the lane, he can attempt to be part of the screen for 3 before curling tightly off of 5's screen.

*   The better the screen that 5 sets, the more open he will be on the slip to the basket.

*   Sequential passing reads are 2, 5, 4, and then 3 as the safety outlet.

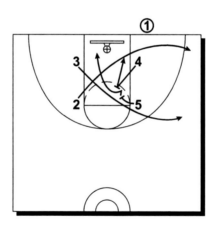

PLAY #6: BOX SET VERSUS A MAN-TO-MAN DEFENSE

Objective: Isolate the post on the block and establish a triangle formation to set up passing angles to take advantage of how he is being defended.

Description: From a box set, 2 starts on the opposite block, 4 on the opposite elbow, 3 on the ballside block, and 5 on the ballside elbow. 2 makes a hard cut to the ballside corner, spotting up on the three-point line. 3 sets a back pick for the post player you are attempting to isolate (5). 5 cuts directly toward the ball, looking for a pass and shot. If a direct pass is denied to 5, he posts up on the block and seals the defender. 3 steps to the ballside wing and reads how the post is being played. 4 flashes to the ballside elbow and reads how 5 is being defended. 1 can inbound the ball to 2 or 3 if 5 is denied, and then cuts back for defensive balance.

Coaching Points:

- If 5's defender trails him on the cut, the pass should go directly to 5 for the shot.

- If a smaller defender switches off on 5, then 2 should look for a direct pass up high to 5.

- If the ball goes to the perimeter, the players should read the post defender and determine who has the best angle to make the entry pass.

- If the defender is on the high side, then the best pass is from 2 in the corner.

- If the defender is behind 5, then the pass can come from 2 or 3.

- If the defender is sealed on the baseline side, then the best passing angle is from 4 at the high post.

- Sequential passing reads are 2, 5, then 3 as the safety outlet.

PLAY #7: BOX SET VERSUS A MAN-TO-MAN DEFENSE

Objective: Screen the screener for a delayed post-up off of a diagonal, little-to-big screen.

Description: Out of a box formation, 5 starts on the opposite block, 3 on the opposite elbow, 2 on the ballside block, and 4 at the ballside elbow. 2 initiates the movement and curls around 4 to get open on the ballside wing. At the same time, 5 sets a screen for 3 to fade to the corner. 3 sets up for 5's screen by V-cutting into the key and then fading to the three-point line. After 1 has inbounded the ball to the wing, he sets a back screen for 5, who cuts directly back to the ball.

Coaching Points:

* The better the screen that 5 sets for 3, the more likely 5 will be open coming off 1's screen.

* After screening for 3, 5 delays slightly before curling off 1.

* If the defender is behind 5 on the block, 2 can make the direct pass to the post.

* If the defender is on the high side of 5, 2 can dribble to the corner to improve his passing angle to 5.

* If the defender is in front or on the baseline side of 5, 2 can pass to 4 at the high post for a high-low feed.

* Sequential passing reads are 2, 5, then 3 as a safety outlet.

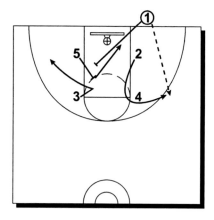

PLAY #8: BOX SET VERSUS A MAN-TO-MAN DEFENSE

Objective: Post up a wing player (3) off of a staggered double-screen.

Description: From a box formation, 3 starts off on the opposite block, 5 on the opposite elbow, 2 on the ball-side block, and 4 on the ball-side elbow. 2 curls up and around 4 to the ball-side wing to receive the inbounds pass. As 2 is curling around, 5 screens down on 3, who has stepped to the outside to receive the screen. 3 then curls toward the ball off of 5, and then off of 1. 1 has come from out-of-bounds to set the final screen. If 3 is not open on the cut, then 2 reads how he is being played in the post and moves appropriately.

Coaching Points:

- As 3 steps out to receive the first screen, he should target the ball with his hands to make his defender honor the cut.

- Once 3 is in the post, he should seal his defender on whichever side he is being played.

- If 3 has his defender behind or on the top side, the feed should be able to come from 2, who can dribble toward the corner if necessary to improve the passing angle.

- If the defender is in front or on the baseline side, then the post entry pass can go to 4 at the high post to make a high-low feed.

- Sequential passing reads are 2, 3.

- 4 needs to be ready to reposition to become the safety outlet.

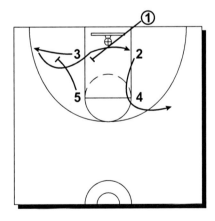

PLAY #9: BOX SET VERSUS A MAN-TO-MAN DEFENSE

Objective: Screen the screener, little to big.

Description: Set up in a box formation with the post (5) on the block opposite the ball and a guard (2)—or the player with the smallest defender—on the ballside block. 5 sets a diagonal screen for 3, who V-cuts and goes hard off the screen. 2 steps in toward the ball and then turns and screens up for 5, who cuts directly toward the ball. After screening, 2 cuts quickly to the three-point line and targets the ball with his hands. 4 can delay and then move anywhere necessary to be a safety outlet.

Coaching Points:

- 3 must step to the outside to set up the screening angle for 5.

- The more solid the screen set by 5, the more of a target his defender is to be screened by 2.

- 5 should not be in a hurry. He needs to wait for the screen from 2.

- As soon as 2 gets solid contact, he needs to explode to the perimeter, spot up on the three-point line, and be ready to catch and shoot.

- Sequential passing reads are 3, 5, 2.

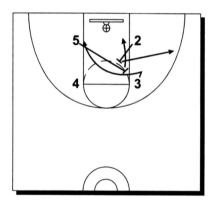

PLAY #10: BOX SET VERSUS A MAN-TO-MAN DEFENSE

Objective: Screen the screener and roll back.

Description: From a box set, 3 starts on the opposite block, 4 on the opposite elbow, 5 on the ballside block, and 2 on the ballside elbow. Place your best shooter (2) on the ballside elbow and the post (5) on the ballside block. 5 begins by screening up for 2, who cuts off the screen to the inside and then circles out to the baseline three-point line. After 5 has set a solid screen, 3 crosses the key and sets a screen on 5's defender at an angle so 5 can cut to the far side of the basket. After screening for 5, 3 rolls back toward the ball, looking for the direct pass. After all the screens and cuts, 4 can move wherever needed to be a safety outlet.

Coaching Points:

- 2 must curl at full speed off of 5 to the corner.
- 3 must search for 5's defender and screen at an angle to get 5 open on the far side of the basket.
- The better the screen 3 sets, the better chance he has to be open on the roll.
- Sequential passing reads are 2, 3, 5 (lob), then 4 as a safety outlet.

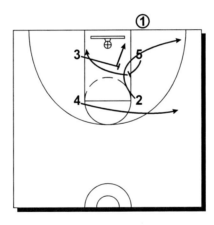

PLAY #11: BOX SET VERSUS A MAN-TO-MAN DEFENSE

Objective: Open on side of the key to screen the screener. Two posts moving toward the ball.

Description: Out of the box formation, 2 starts on the opposite block, 3 lines up on the opposite elbow, 4 on the ballside block, and 5 on the ballside elbow. 2 and 3 cut hard off of the screeners (4 and 5) to the three-point line on the ballside. 5 steps toward 3 to screen and 4 holds his position on the block to let 2 rub off. After 2 and 3 have cut off the screens, 4 sets a back pick for 5 to come directly to the ball and then rolls off the screen to the far side of the key.

Coaching Points:

- 2 and 3 should not run straight-line cuts, but need to set up with a step low if they want to cut on the high side or a step high if they want to cut on the low side.

- 5 must step toward 3 to set the screen to allow a good screening angle for 4 on the back pick.

- The more solidly 4 screens 5's defender, the more likely it is that 4 will be open on the roll.

- Sequential passing reads are 2, 5, 4, then 3 as the safety outlet.

PLAY #12: BOX SET VERSUS A MAN-TO-MAN DEFENSE

Objective: Clear a side of the key for a quick post or tip pass back to the inbounder.

Description: From a box formation, 2 and 3 step into the key and then X-cut across the key to the ballside, off 4 and 5. 3 starts high and goes under 4 to the three-point line, and 2 starts low and goes over the top of 5 to the three-point line. 5 then immediately clears to the opposite side of the floor to clear out for the following action. After 3 has cleared 4's screen, 4 posts up and calls for the ball. 4's defender should be on the baseline side, allowing the ball to be thrown over the top. 4 should have a shot on the catch unless 1's defender has come to help. If 1's defender has come over to help, 1 should go directly to the far side of the basket and 4 can quickly return the ball to 1 with a touch pass or tip. The quicker the ball gets out of 4's hands, the more effective the play will be.

Coaching Points:

- The harder and tighter that 3 cuts off 4, the more likely it is that 4 will have space to pass toward.

- 4 should set the screen for 3 below the level of the block to create more space above him to receive the ball.

- If 4's defender for some reason gets caught on the high side, the inbound pass can go directly to 4.

- As 1 lobs the ball over 4's defender, he should quickly read his own defender. If his defender stays on him, 1 can move to the opposite corner to clear the space for 4.

- If 1's defender moves over to help on the lob to 4, 1 should quickly move to the far side of the basket and expect the ball to be quickly tipped back to him.

- If possible, the tip should be made high, so 1 can catch and shoot immediately without coming back to the floor.

- Sequential passing reads are 4-to-1, 3, 2, and then 5 as the safety outlet.

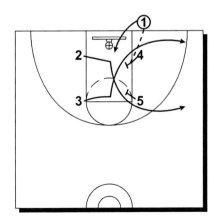

PLAY #13: BOX SET VERSUS A MAN-TO-MAN DEFENSE

Objective: Isolate single cutter on an open side of the floor with a screen and rescreen.

Description: This play is a companion play for Play #11. Using a box formation, 2 starts on the opposite block, 3 on the opposite elbow, 4 on the ballside block, and 5 on the ballside elbow. 2 and 3 both cut hard toward the ballside. 2 cuts off 4's screen a step outside the key. 3 cuts hard over the top side of 5's screen, then quickly reverses direction and cuts back over the top of 5, then cuts right back down the open side of the key. After screening the second time, 5 pops out to the perimeter as a safety outlet.

Coaching Points:

- 1's sequential reads are 2, ball fake to 3 on the outside, and 3 on the return cut.

- 2 must cut hard and call for the ball.

- 4 sets the screen a step outside the key in order to keep the key area open for 3's second cut.

- 5 lets 3 come to him on the first cut to give 3 more room on his return cut, and then searches hard for a solid contact screen as 3 returns.

- Sequential passing reads are 2, 3, 4, then 5 as the safety outlet.

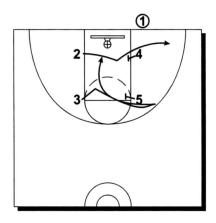

PLAY #14: BOX SET VERSUS A MAN-TO-MAN DEFENSE

Objective: Circle cut to defeat a defender who is overplaying the shooter. Step out jumper for the screener and basket cut for the post.

Description: This play is a companion play for Plays #11 and #13. From a box formation, 2 starts on the opposite block, 3 on the opposite elbow, 4 on the ballside block, and 5 on the ballside elbow. 2 and 3 begin their cuts simultaneously. 3 cuts hard past 5's screen. 2 cuts hard under the screen of 4, then quickly reverses direction and circles back over the top of 4, returning toward the basket and the open side of the key. After 2 circles 4, 4 pops back out to a shooting position on the baseline. 5 delays until 2 has cleared the circle cut, and then cuts directly down the lane line toward the ball.

Coaching Points:

- 4 pops backward to the perimeter in a shooting position.

- 5 delays and decoys his defender, then makes his cut after the low block on his side is cleared. He then makes a hard direct basket cut toward the ball.

- 1's sequential reads are ball fake toward 2's cut to the corner, 2 as he curls back to the basket, 4 as he pops out to the perimeter, and finally 5 as he slips down the lane directly toward the ball.

PLAY #15: BOX SET VERSUS A MAN-TO-MAN DEFENSE

Objective: Staggered, double-screen for the inbounder.

Description: From a box formation, 4 starts on the opposite block, 5 on the opposite elbow, 2 on the ballside block, and 3 on the ballside elbow. 2 sets an up screen for 3, who has V-cut into the key before coming off 2's screen and cutting toward the baseline three-point line. After 2 screens, he immediately clears to the opposite wing beyond the three-point line. After 1 has inbounded the ball to 3, he circles away and receives a screen from 4 at the bottom of the key and then from 5 in the middle of the key. 1 comes off the two screens and cuts to the three-point line, looking to receive a pass from 3.

Coaching Points:

- 3 must get open off of 2's screen. He can go as wide as necessary to receive the ball.

- After receiving the ball, 3's sequential reads are drive, pass to 4 on the block, 1 coming off the staggered double, and then skip pass to 2 on the opposite three-point line.

- If 4's man hedges to help on 1's cut on the top, 4 should pin him on the high side and call for the ball from 3.

- After screening, 5 should read where the pass is made, anticipate a shot, and move to the correct rebounding angle.

- Sequential passing reads are 3, 4, 1, then 2 as the safety outlet.

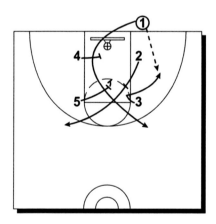

PLAY #16: BOX SET VERSUS A MAN-TO-MAN DEFENSE

Objective: Staggered double-screen for the best shooter, quick post, and post slip.

Description: From a box formation, 3 starts on the opposite block, 2 on the opposite elbow, 5 on the ballside block, and 4 on the ballside elbow. 4 and 5 both head toward 2 to set screens. As 5 leaves, 3 makes a direct, hard cut toward the ball, stopping at the low block. 2 V-cuts away and comes back off of a screen set by 4 and then a second one set by 5, cutting toward the three-point line on the ballside baseline. After screening for 2, 4 slips down to the backside block and 5 flares to the wing as a safety outlet.

Coaching Points:

- 4 and 5 must search for solid contact on 2's defender.

- 1 must read if the defense is switching or getting screened.

- Before 3 cuts, he should decoy his man by acting as if he is going to screen up or not be involved in the play.

- 1's sequential reads are 3 on his cut toward the ball, 2 coming off the staggered double-screen, 4 on the slip down the backside of the key, and then 5 as a safety outlet.

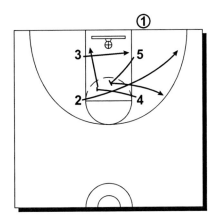

PLAY #17: BOX SET VERSUS A MAN-TO-MAN DEFENSE

Objective: Screen and rescreen, big and little. One pass for a shot.

Description: From a box formation, 3 starts on the opposite block, 4 on the opposite elbow, 2 on the ballside block, and 5 on the ballside elbow. 2 and 3 set simultaneous screens up and across for 4 and 5. 4 and 5 cut hard off the screen toward the box opposite from where they started looking for the direct pass. If they do not receive the inbound pass, they take a step outside the key and screen for 2 and 3, who are circling to the outside and then back toward the ball. 2 screens up and across for 4, then circles to the outside and cuts off 5's screen. 3 screens up and across for 5, then circles to the outside and comes back around 4's screen to the ball.

Coaching Points:

- 4 and 5 must wait for the first screen to arrive, then cut off, looking for the direct pass. Even if they do not receive the direct pass, they will make the defense honor the position at the block.

- By stepping outside the key (at lease one large step), 4 and 5 are allowing room for 2 and 3 to get themselves open as they come around the outside and cut back toward the ball.

- After setting the second screen, 4 can step out and become the safety outlet.

- Sequential passing reads are 4, 5, 3, 2, then 4 as the safety outlet.

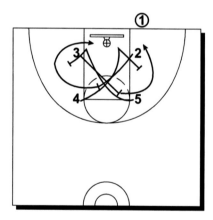

PLAY #18: BOX SET VERSUS A MAN-TO-MAN DEFENSE

Objective: Use the inbounder to screen little to big. Two passes for a shot.

Description: Out of a box formation, 4 starts on the opposite block, 2 on the opposite elbow, 5 on the ballside block, and 3 at the ballside elbow. 5 posts up and then quickly pops out to the corner to receive the inbound pass from 1. After passing, 1 screens for 4. 4 comes off the screen and looks for a direct pass or a post-up on the pass from 5.

Coaching Points:

- For 5 to get open on the pop out, he needs to first step into his defender.

- When 1 still has the ball, 4 should step slightly out to the perimeter to begin setting up his man to receive the screen from 1.

- If 1 gets a solid screen and no switch occurs, then 4 should be open for a direct pass and a score.

- If 1 gets a solid screen that forces a switch, then 4 should look to post up the smaller defender on the block.

- Sequential passing reads are 1 to 5 to 4.

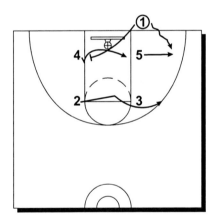

PLAY #19: BOX SET VERSUS A MAN-TO-MAN DEFENSE

Objective: Three passes for a shot.

Description: This play can be used as a continuation of Play #18 when the options to 4 are not available. From a box set, 4 starts on the opposite block, 2 on the opposite elbow, 5 on the ballside block, and 3 on the ballside elbow. After 5 has popped out and received the inbound pass from 1 and 1 has set the screen for 4, if 4 is not open for either the direct pass and shot or the post-up, then 3 should pop to the perimeter on the ballside wing and receive the pass from 5. 1 reads that the ball is passed to 3 and sets a back pick for 2, who comes off looking for the lob or direct pass and score.

Coaching Points:

- 1 and 3 must make a quick read to see if 4 is going to receive the direct pass from 5 or get the ball on the mismatch post-up.

- 3 steps into his defender and then pops to the perimeter.

- 1 looks to set a solid screen on 2's defender.

- 2 decoys his defender and then comes off the back screen hard and tight, looking for the lob or direct pass on the cut.

- Sequential passing reads are 5-to-4, then 5-to-3-to-2 or -1.

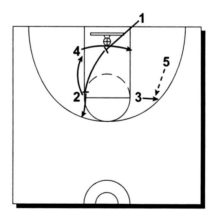

PLAY #20: BOX SET VERSUS A MAN-TO-MAN DEFENSE

Objective: Three passes for a shot.

Description: This play can be used as a continuation option from Play #18, with the inbounder coming off a staggered double-screen. From the box set described in Play #19, 1 inbounds the ball to 5 and sets a screen for 4 (Diagram 20a). If 1 is a good shooter, you can use this play to get the ball back to him. After receiving the ball and reading 4 coming off the screen, 5 passes the ball to 3, who has popped to the perimeter. When 3 receives the ball, 4 immediately turns and screens for 1. 1 comes off 4's screen and then off a screen set by 5. 5 sets the screen immediately after 4 (Diagram 20b).

Coaching Points:

- This play may be the primary option if 1 is a great shooter.

- 1 can cut on the low side of both screens or curl over and under the screens.

- 4 tries to get his screen set in the middle of the key.

- 5 tries to set his screen as close to the side of the key as possible so 1 has more room to get open.

- Sequential passing reads are 1 to 5 to 3 to 1.

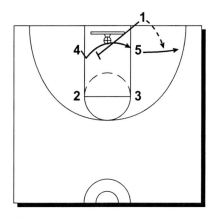

Diagram 20a

Diagram 20b

PLAY #21: BOX SET VERSUS A MAN-TO-MAN DEFENSE

Objective: Isolate the post who is inbounding the ball with either a direct return pass or a high-low feed. Two or three passes for a shot.

Description: From a box formation, use your best post player (5) to inbound the ball. The other post lines up on the block on the side opposite the ball. 2 pops out of the box to the perimeter on the baseline. As soon as 2 receives the ball, 5 cuts hard and posts up on the block, looking for a direct pass back from 2. At the same time, both 1 and 3 set a double-screen for 4, who cuts toward the elbow on the ballside. 2 either passes the ball directly to 5 on the block or to 4 at the elbow for a high-low entry pass to 5.

Coaching Points:

- After inbounding the ball, 5 tries to hook his defender and get him caught directly behind him so he can receive a pass from 2.

- 2 must read how 5 is being played. If 5's defender is fronting or playing him on the low side, the pass should go to 4, who has the better passing angle to 5 on a high-low feed.

- 1 and 3 can set a double-screen or a staggered double-screen to get 4 open at the high post.

- After setting the screen for 4, both 1 and 3 must clear to the perimeter to take their defenders away and operate one-on-one. This move will open up the low post area so 5 can receive the pass from either 2 or 4.

- Sequential passing reads are 1-to-2-to-5, then 1-to-2-to-4-to-5.

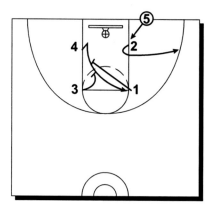

PLAY #22: BOX SET VERSUS A MAN-TO-MAN DEFENSE

Objective: Triple screen for inbounder. Two passes for a shot.

Description: This play is designed for a great shooter inbounding the ball. From a box formation, 3 starts on the opposite block, 4 on the opposite elbow, 2 on the ballside block, and 5 on the ballside elbow. 2 pops to the perimeter and receives the inbound pass from 1. As soon as the ball is inbounded, 3 sets a screen on 1's defender as 1 cuts away from his pass. Then 4 sets a screen for 1 to begin curling up toward the free-throw-line area. Finally, 5 sets the third screen for 1 to curl back toward the wing on the ballside. 2 reads the screens and looks to hit either 1 coming off the third screen or one of the screeners (3, 4, or 5) who is slipping to the basket.

Coaching Points:

- If 1's defender gets caught on the first screen, the ball can be thrown over the top to 1 at the basket.

- The second and third screens need to be set at angles to get the shooter (1) open for a perimeter jumper.

- 1 needs to cut hard and tight off the screens and be ready to catch and shoot.

- All three screeners can look to slip their screen if their defender hedges too far to help on the cutter.

- Sequential passing reads are 1-to-2-to-1 or -3 at the post.

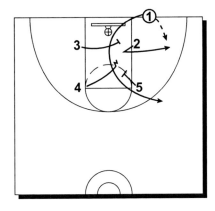

PLAY #23: BOX SET VERSUS A MAN-TO-MAN DEFENSE

Objective: Screen the screener little to big and roll back. One pass for a shot.

Description: From a box formation, 4 starts on the opposite block, 3 on the opposite elbow, 2 on the ballside block, and 5 on the ballside elbow. 4 pops to the perimeter away from the ball and 5 starts with a screen on 3's defender. 3 cuts over the top to the wing on the ballside of the floor. After 5 has set the screen for 3, 2 screens up on 5's defender and then rolls quickly back to the basket.

Coaching Points:

- The better the screen 5 sets for 3, the better chance 5 has to be open coming off 2's screen.

- If 2's defender switches onto 5, 5 should post up and call for the ball.

- 4 should get to the three-point line and target the ball.

- 2 must get solid contact on the screen before slipping the screen to the basket.

- 3 can be the safety outlet.

- Sequential passing reads are 4 (if left open), 5, 2, and 3 as the safety.

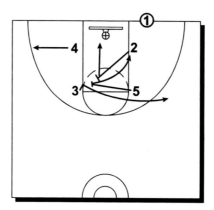

PLAY #24: BOX SET VERSUS A MAN-TO-MAN DEFENSE

Objective: Diagonal back screens with little screening big. One pass for a shot.

Description: From a box formation, 3 starts on the opposite block, 5 on the opposite elbow, 2 on the ballside block, and 4 on the ballside elbow. 3 starts with a screen for 4 and then flares to the ballside wing. 4 comes off 3's screen and cuts to the corner to look for the perimeter shot and also to clear the key area for the second screen on 5. 2 delays slightly to let 3 and 4 make their cuts and then screens up on 5's defender. 5 cuts off the screen directly down the key toward the ball.

Coaching Points:

• Both 4 and 5 can set up their defenders for the screens by moving slightly to the outside.

• After 3 screens for 4, he quickly slips to the outside and should be open if his defender helps at all on 4's cut.

• 2 needs to set the screen for 5 at an angle so that 5 can cut directly down the key.

• 2 should wait until 4 is just clearing the key to begin moving up to set the screen for 5.

• Sequential passing reads are 4, 3, 5, and 2 as a safety outlet.

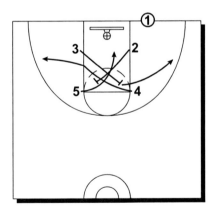

2

1-4 Low Sets

PLAY #25: 1-4 LOW SET VERSUS A MAN-TO-MAN DEFENSE

Objective: Cross screen and roll back from fake screen. One pass for a shot.

Description: From a 1-4 low set, 5 starts in the opposite corner, 3 on the opposite block, 4 on the ballside block, and 2 in the ballside corner. 4 screens across for 3. 3 cuts off the screen toward the ball. 3 continues out to set a potential screen on 5's defender, and then quickly reverses direction and cuts hard back toward the basket. 5 goes over the top of the fake screen and becomes the safety outlet. 2 stays spotted up on the three-point line.

Coaching Points:

- Place a good shooter in the 2 spot so that they must be defended and keep the key clear.

- 4 needs to set a solid first screen before heading out toward 5.

- The quicker 4 can change direction, the more difficult this play will be to defend.

- Sequential passing reads are 2 (if left open), 3, 4, and then 5.

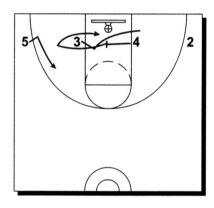

PLAY #26: 1-4 LOW SET VERSUS A MAN-TO-MAN DEFENSE

Objective: Screen for a cutter coming toward the ball and then read the defender of the screener. One pass for a shot.

Description: From a 1-4 low set, 3 starts in the opposite corner, 5 on the opposite block, 2 on the ballside block, and 4 in the ballside corner. 4 spots up on the three-point line. 2 starts on the ballside block and quickly cuts away from the ball under 5. 5 sets a screen for 3, who is cutting off the screen toward the basket. If 5's defender moves to help on 3's cut, 5 should be open for a direct pass and shot.

Coaching Points:

- 2 sets up his cut to the corner by making his preliminary move high and then cutting low under 5.

- 5 really doesn't screen for 2 as much as 2 cuts off him.

- 5 establishes his position about four feet off the lane to give 3 more open space around the basket.

- 3 starts his cut by going low and then cutting hard over the top of 5, directly toward the basket.

- 5 screens for 3 with his back so he can see both the ball and his defender.

- If 5 gets a solid screen on 3's defender and pins him on his back, then 5's defender must move with 3 toward the basket to help on 3's cut. As a result, 5 should have an open cut to the basket for a direct pass.

- 1 reads 5's defender. If he stays, 3 should be open. If he moves with 3, then 5 should have the new defender on his back and be open.

- Sequential passing reads are ball fake to 2, 3, 5, and then 4 as the safety outlet.

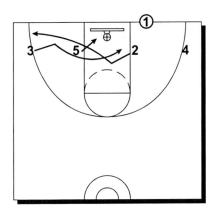

PLAY #27: 1-4 LOW SET VERSUS A MAN-TO-MAN DEFENSE

Objective: Screen, rescreen, and post up. One pass for a shot.

Description: From a 1-4 low set, 2 starts in the opposite corner, 4 on the opposite block, 5 on the ballside block, and 3 in the ballside corner. Place a shooter (3) in the ballside corner so that he has to be checked and it keeps the key open. 5 pops to the elbow on the ballside to clear the key area for the following action. 2 cuts hard over the top of 4, gets to the middle of the key, and then receives a return screen from 4 to cut back to the three-point line. 4 sets the first screen from a step outside the key and then follows 2 into the cut and screens in on 2 to get open for a shot on the three-point line. On both screens, 4 looks for a chance to slip to the basket for a direct pass and shot.

Coaching Points:

- 3 should spot up on the three-point line, ready to receive a pass any time his defender sags to help on the cuts in the key.

- 4 begins a step outside the key to give 2 more open space in the key.

- 2 cuts hard over the top of 4 toward the ball, looking for a direct pass and shot.

- 4 should set the initial screen with his back so he has vision of the ball and of his defender.

- As soon as 2 has made the first cut into the key and neither 4 nor 2 has received the pass, 4 screens into the key for 2.

- After screening the second time, 4 looks for a chance to slip the screen if his defender moves to help at all on 2's cut.

- Sequential passing reads are 2, 4 on the first cut; 2, 4 on the second cut; and 5 or 3 as the safety outlet.

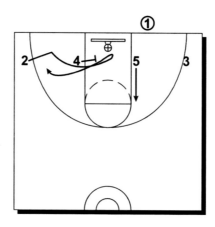

PLAY #28: 1-4 LOW SET VERSUS A MAN-TO-MAN DEFENSE

Objective: Cross cut and double-screen for the best shooter. One pass for a shot.

Description: From a 1-4 low set, 4 starts in the opposite corner, 2 on the opposite block, 5 on the ballside post, and 3 in the ballside corner. Place your strongest shooter (2) on the block opposite the ball. The play begins with 3 cutting off 5 into the key, looking for a direct pass. After clearing 5 into the key, if 3 does not receive the ball, he sets a screen for 2. 2 cuts over the top of 3's screen and then continues by going under a screen set by 5 on his way to the three-point line in the corner. 5 looks to slip the screen and receive a pass if his defender moves to help on either 3 or 2 as they cut.

Coaching Points:

- 2 delays his cut until 3 has cleared 5 and is in the key, giving 3 a chance to get open and receive the first pass.

- While waiting to cut, 2 can back up slightly from the key to create more space.

- 3 sets the screen for 2 as far across the key as possible to give 2 room to maneuver.

- After cutting over the top of 3, 2 circles under 5 toward the three-point line for a shot.

- 5 screens 3 with his back and then 2 with his front, so that he is constantly in sight of the ball.

- 3, as the safety outlet, can peel back out to the ballside wing.

- Sequential passing reads are 3, 5, 2, 5, and then 3 as the safety outlet.

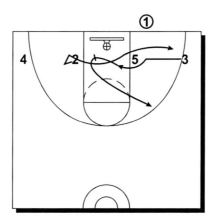

PLAY #29: 1-4 LOW SET VERSUS A MAN-TO-MAN DEFENSE

Objective: Triple-screen for best shooter (2). One pass for a shot.

Description: This play is a companion play for Play #28. Use the same 1-4 alignment described for Play #28. In this play, the best shooter (2) starts in the corner opposite the ball with the posts (4 and 5) on the blocks. 3 initiates the movement with a quick cut over the top of 5 into the middle of the key, looking for a direct pass and shot. As 3 is entering the key area, 2 begins his cut with a V-cut high and then cuts under 4's screen, over 3's screen, and under 5's screen. After screening, 4, 3, and 5 all look for a chance to slip the screen if their defender moves to help. 2 is not really looking for the pass and shot until he gets to the far corner after all three screens.

Coaching Points:

- As 3 enters the key, 2 should already begin his preliminary V-cut.

- 2 must cut hard, circling under, over, and then under the three screens.

- 4 should set the first screen with his back while facing the ball so he can have vision of the ball and his defender.

- 3 and 5 should work to get solid contact before looking to slip to the basket.

- 3 can peel back out to the ballside wing as the safety outlet.

- Sequential passing reads are 2 all the way, with the only exception being if one of the defenders on the screeners moves way out of position to help, and then 3 as the safety outlet.

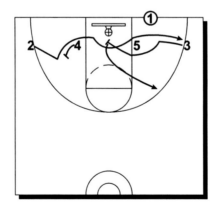

PLAY #30: 1-4 LOW SET VERSUS A MAN-TO-MAN DEFENSE

Objective: Triple-screen for the best shooter (2) with a predetermined slip. One pass for a shot.

Description: This play is a companion play for Plays #28 and #29. The play starts from a 1-4 low set with the posts (4 and 5) on the blocks and the best shooter (2) in the corner opposite the ball. All four players begin the movement at the same time. 4 steps out to set the first screen for 2, followed by 5, who moves across the key. 3 starts by cutting high and then screening at a down angle for 2. 2 cuts over 4 and then under both 5 and 3, while cutting up and out to the ballside wing. 3 sets the final screen higher in the key and then slips the screen toward the ball, looking for a direct pass and shot. If 3 is not open on the slip, he can move to the ballside corner as the safety outlet.

Coaching Points:

- This play should look very similar to Play #29 at the beginning.

- 4 and 5 try to create as much operating room as possible by moving toward 2 to set their screens.

- 3 starts by moving high, so he can set a screen in above the block and have room to slip the screen to the basket.

- The harder 2 cuts off the screens, the better chance 3 has to be open on the slip.

- If 3 is not open, he can cut back out to the ballside corner as the safety outlet.

- Sequential passing reads are ball fake to 2 after the final screen, and then 3 on the slip to the basket.

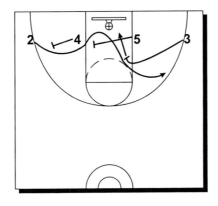

PLAY #31: 1-4 LOW SET VERSUS A MAN-TO-MAN DEFENSE

Objective: Post-to-post cross screen for a direct pass and shot.

Description: This play is a companion play for Plays #29 and #30. From a 1-4 low set, the posts (4 and 5) start at the blocks with 2 and 3 in the corners. 2 starts with a cut off of 4, similar to Plays #29 and #30. 2 cuts on the low side of 4 and then immediately cuts to the ballside elbow. As 2 clears 4's screen, 5 looks like he is going to set the same screen for 2, but instead he sets a cross screen for 4. 4 decoys as if he is doing the same job as he did in Play #30, then comes off 5's screen hard to the ball. After screening, 5 turns and faces the ball, looking for a pass if the defenders switch. 2 and 3 can operate as the safety outlets.

Coaching Points:

- 2 and 4 need to make this play look exactly like Plays #29 and #30.

- 4 should decoy that his only job is to set the screen for 2, and then cut hard off of 5's screen.

- 5 should decoy that he is moving to set a screen for 2, and then get solid contact with 4's defender.

- If the defenders don't switch, 4 should be open. If they do switch, then 5 should be able to pin the defender and roll back to the ball.

- 3 should spot up on the three-point line, ready to receive the pass and shoot if his defender sags to help in the key.

- Sequential passing reads are 4, 5, and then 2 or 3 as the safety outlet.

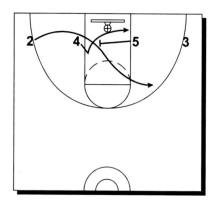

PLAY #32: 1-4 LOW SET VERSUS A MAN-TO-MAN DEFENSE

Objective: Screen and roll, post to post. One pass for a shot.

Description: From a 1-4 low set, 2 starts in the opposite corner, 4 on the opposite block, 5 on the ballside block, and 3 in the ballside corner. 2 and 3 spot up on the three-point line in case either of their defenders sags to help in the key. 5 begins the movement by popping out to the ballside elbow and calling for the ball. As 5 gets to the elbow, 4 sets a screen on the baseline side of his defender and 5 cuts hard to the block on the opposite side of the ball. After screening for 5, 4 rolls back to the ball, looking for a direct pass and shot.

Coaching Points:

- 5 backpedals out to the elbow and targets the ball.

- 4 must set the screen at an angle to get 5 open at the opposite block.

- 4 then pivots to pin the defender on his back and rolls back down the key directly toward the ball.

- 2 and 3 can move wherever necessary to be safety outlets.

- Sequential passing reads are 5, 4, and then 2 or 3 as the safety outlet.

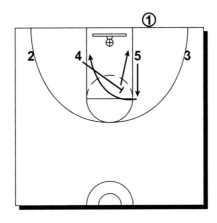

PLAY #33: 1-4 LOW SET VERSUS A MAN-TO-MAN DEFENSE

Objective: High-low pass, post to post to take advantage of denial position of the defender. Two passes for a shot.

Description: This play is designed to take advantage of a defender who is denying a direct pass to the post by playing on the baseline side. Start from a 1-4 low set with the posts (4 and 5) at the blocks and 2 and 3 in the corners. 5 pops quickly to the ballside elbow and receives the inbound pass from 1. As 5 receives the ball, his first look is to 4, who should have his defender pinned on the low side and should be able to catch the ball close to the basket and score. 2 and 3 spot up on the three-point line and look for the direct pass and shot if their defenders sag to help in the key.

Coaching Points:

- To help create space, 4 should move toward the ball, forcing his defender to deny his cut and stay on the baseline side.

- 5 steps into his defender and then explodes to the elbow to receive the inbound pass.

- As soon as 5 catches the ball, he needs to anticipate 4 having his defender pinned on the baseline side, and look for an immediate high-low pass.

- 2 and 3 can move wherever necessary to be safety outlets.

- Sequential passing reads are 1-to-5, 5-to-4, and then 2 or 3 for the safety outlet.

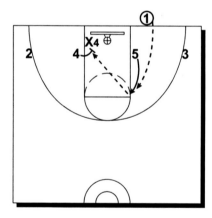

PLAY #34: 1-4 LOW SET VERSUS A MAN-TO-MAN DEFENSE

Objective: Little screening big, lob or roll. One pass for a shot.

Description: From a 1-4 low set, 2 lines up on the baseline three-point line opposite the ball. 5 is at the block opposite the ball. 4 clears the key by popping to the ballside elbow, and 3 spots up on the three-point line, ready to catch and shoot if his defender drops to the key area to help. 5 steps across the key toward the ball at the same time that 2 cuts in toward the key. 2 sets a back screen on 5's defender. 5 peels back around the screen, looking for the lob if his defender was picked off or if the smaller defender switched onto him. After setting the screen for 5, 2 slips to the open area of the key looking for the direct pass and shot.

Coaching Points:

- As 5 makes his initial move toward the ball, he must target the ball with his hands to force his defender to deny the cut.

- 2 sets the screen from behind and at an angle that allows 5 to peel over the top to look for the lob or the mismatch.

- 4 clears the key and calls for the ball if his defender stays to help in the key.

- Sequential passing reads are 5 on the direct cut, 5 peeling off the screen, 2 slipping the screen, and then 3 or 4 as a safety outlet.

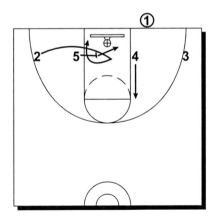

PLAY #35: 1-4 LOW SET VERSUS A MAN-TO-MAN DEFENSE

Objective: Screen the screener, little to big—all four players moving. One pass for a shot.

Description: From a 1-4 low set, the posts (4 and 5) start on the blocks and 2 and 3 set up on the corner three-point lines. 4 and 2 set the first screens. 4 steps out from the key to screen for 3, who cuts off the screen on the low side toward the basket. 4 screens with his back so he can face the ball and his defender. If his defender switches, 4 can pin 3's defender on his back and receive a direct pass for a shot. 3 stops on the opposite-side block unless he can receive a direct pass to score. At the same time, 2 screens down for 5 on the ballside block. 5 cuts off the screen to the corner and targets the ball. After screening for 5, 2 moves across the key and screens for 4. 4 cuts off the screen and moves across the key to the ballside block, attempting to leave his defender on the screen or simply beat him across the key.

Coaching Points:

• 1 needs to be alert to early possibilities—3 coming off 4's screen and 4 pinning and cutting to the basket if the defense switches.

• 2 needs to move quickly across the key to make his second screen.

• Unless he has a direct pass and shot, 3 stops at the block opposite the ball to keep the rest of the key open for 4.

• After the second screen, 2 can cut back across the key to the ballside wing as the safety outlet.

• Sequential passing reads are 3 coming off 4's screen, 4 on the slip, and 4 coming off 2's screen.

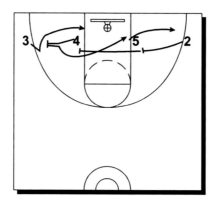

PLAY #36: 1-4 LOW SET VERSUS A MAN-TO-MAN OR ZONE DEFENSE

Objective: Clear the key and screen for the inbounder, little screening big. Two passes for a shot.

Description: From a 1-4 low set, have your best scoring post (4) inbound the ball. The other post (5) lines up on the ballside block. 1 and 2 spot up in the corner and call for the ball if their defenders move to help in the key. 5 pops out to the ballside elbow and receives the inbound pass. As 5 catches the ball, 4 takes a step into the key to set up for the screen from 2. 2 screens down on 4's defender at an angle to allow 4 to cut to the outside of the screen and curl over the top to receive the high-low pass from 5. 2 should immediately pop back out to the corner, giving 4 room to operate and putting himself in position to receive the pass from 5 in case 4's defender beats him over the top and is playing him on the high side, denying the pass from 5 to 4. From his position in the corner, 2 has a better passing angle to make the feed to 4, who must pin and hold the defender on the high side to receive the pass from 3 in the corner.

Coaching Points:

- 5 must step into his defender toward the ball and then quickly explode off him to get open at the ballside elbow.

- 4 must step into the key to give 2 a better chance to set a solid screen.

- 2 must set the screen at an angle to allow 4 to cut over the top and curl into the key.

- 5 must read how 4 is being played as he comes off the screen and decide if he has a direct pass or if he should pass to 2 returning to the corner. A defender on the top side is the key to pass the ball to 2.

- If the defender is on the top of 4, 4 moves up the lane line to create more space and provide a better entry pass angle for 2 or 5.

- Sequential passing reads are inbound to 5, then 5-to-4 or 5-to-2-to-4.

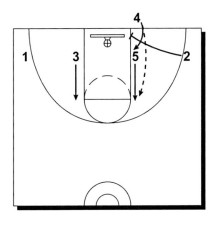

PLAY #37: 1-4 LOW SET VERSUS A MAN-TO-MAN DEFENSE

Objective: Double-screen for the inbounder. Two passes for a shot.

Description: This play is a companion play for Play #36. From a 1-4 low set, the posts (4 and 5) set up on the blocks with 2 and 3 in the corners. 5 pops back to the ballside elbow to receive the inbound pass. As soon as 5 receives the ball, 4 screens on 1's defender to get 1 open cutting to the opposite side, away from the pass. 2 sets a second screen for 1 as he continues to curl off the screens to the wing or elbow, depending on how he is defended. 5 makes the pass to 1 and moves to the offensive boards, anticipating a shot. 5 can also look for 4 slipping the screen or moving across the key to the ballside block, looking for a high-low entry pass. If 1 is not open coming off the double-screen, 5 can pass to 4. If 4's defender is on the top side, as he should be, 5 can pass to 3 in the corner. 3 will have the best angle to enter the ball to 4, who needs to pin and hold his defender on the top side.

Coaching Points:

• 5 must step into his defender, toward the ball, before quickly exploding to the ballside elbow to receive the inbound pass.

• 1 delays slightly and steps into his defender to set up the screens from 4 and 2.

• 4 and 2 must set separate screens at angles to allow 1 to fade toward the wing or curl to the elbow.

• If 1's defender goes under the screens, 1 can fade to the wing.

• If 1's defender follows over the top of the screens, 1 should curl back around toward the elbow to receive the pass from 5.

• If 1 is not open, 5's next read is to 4 posting up on the ballside block.

• Sequential passing reads are inbound to 5, 5-to–1, 5-to-4 on the slip of the screen, 5-to-4 (high-low), or 5-to-3-to-4.

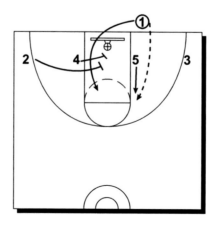

PLAY #38: 1-4 LOW SET VERSUS A MAN-TO-MAN DEFENSE

Objective: Inbound, into a flex cut and flex continuity, beginning with a little screening big. Three passes for a shot.

Description: From a 1-4 low set, 5 starts on the ballside low block and 4 is in the corner. 1 makes the inbound pass to 5 as he pops out to the ballside elbow. 2 immediately steps into his defender and pops to the opposite elbow to receive the pass from 5. As 2 receives the pass, 1 steps in to fill an empty spot on the block and screens for 4, who is executing a flex cut into the key and looking for the return pass from 2. If 4 is not open, then the five-man flex continuity offense can be run beginning with 5 screening down for 1.

Coaching Points:

- 5 must step into his defender to set up his pop out to the elbow to receive the inbound pass.

- 2 must step into his defender to set up his cut to the opposite elbow to receive the pass from 5.

- 2 must read the defenders on the screen that 1 sets for a cutting 4. If 1 gets a solid screen on 4's defender, and 4 is open, then 2 should pass directly to 4 for a shot. If the defenders switch, then 4 should have mismatch and work hard to receive a high-low pass in the post area.

- If 4 is not open, then 5 should immediately screen down for 1 and the flex continuity pattern should begin.

- Sequential passing reads are inbound to 5, 5 passes to 2, 2 reads the flex cut by 4 and passes to 4, then 1 coming up off the screen by 5.

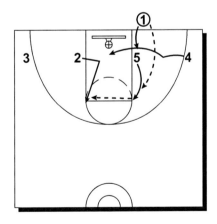

3

Stack Sets

PLAY #39: STACK SET VERSUS A MAN-TO-MAN OR ZONE DEFENSE

Objective: Working in partners. Big screening little and little screening big. One pass for a shot.

Description: From a stack position, players line up, alternating small and big (3, 4, 2, 5). 3 cuts quickly to the outside and targets the ball so his defender has to honor the cut. 4 immediately steps out and sets a back screen for 3, who cuts hard off the screen to the basket. After screening for 3, 4 should turn and face the ball to counter a defensive switch. 5 delays to let both 3 and 4 clear the key and then 5 cuts directly off 2 toward the ball. After screening for 5, 2 can step to the wing and be a safety outlet.

Coaching Points:

- 3 should step into his defender prior to cutting hard to the outside.

- By targeting the ball with his hands and voice, 3 forces his defender to stay close enough to deny a direct pass and therefore is easier to screen.

- 4 can step out and set the back screen with his back so he can see how his defender helps on the cut. On a switch, 4 should keep 3's defender on his back and target the ball.

- If 5 reads that 4 has a defender on his back, he anticipates the pass going to 4 and waits on his cut toward the ball.

- 2 and 5 can decoy their defenders by relaxing for a count while 3 and 4 cut and screen. As they are clearing the key, 5 cuts hard, directly toward the ball. If fronted or switched, 5 can take the defender low to the baseline and call for the pass to come over the top.

- After 5 has cleared, 2 can move to the wing to become the safety outlet.

- Sequential passing reads are 3 stepping out to the perimeter, 3 coming off 4's screen, 4 after setting the screen, 5 cutting down the lane, then 2 as the safety outlet.

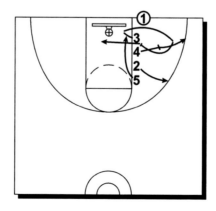

PLAY #40: STACK SET VERSUS A MAN-TO-MAN OR ZONE DEFENSE

Objective: Quick post-up, and then little screening big. One pass for a shot.

Description: From a stack alignment, alternating little, big (3, 5, 2, 4), the play begins with a good shooter (3) popping to the corner three-point line, either being open or dragging his defender with him to open up the lane. 5 immediately fills the low spot by taking his defender as low to the baseline as possible. If 5's defender is mismatched or stays low on the baseline side, then 5 can receive a pass over the top of the defender. As 5 is moving his defender toward the baseline, 4 steps to the outside and calls for the ball. 2 steps to the inside to prepare for the correct screening angle. 4 then cuts off 2's screen toward the backside of the basket. If the two defenders switch the screen, 4 should have a mismatch. 2 can cut to the wing to become the safety outlet.

Coaching Points:

- 3 must quickly cut to the three-point line and call for the ball if open.

- 5 can move as close to the ball as possible if his defender is on the baseline side.

- The play can be run specifically for 5 if a mismatch or quick post opportunity occurs.

- As 4 steps to the outside to set up the screen, he should call for the ball with his voice and hands.

- 2 steps to the inside and sets a screen at an angle to get 4 open on the block, opposite the ball.

- Sequential passing reads are 3 popping out to the three-point line, over the top to 5 on the quick post, 4 cutting off 2's screen, and then 2 on the wing as the safety outlet.

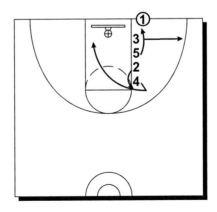

PLAY #41: STACK SET VERSUS A MAN-TO-MAN DEFENSE

Objective: Small to big screen, leading to a quick post isolation, from the second pass. Two passes for a post-up or shot.

Description: From a stack alignment, alternating small, big (2, 4, 3, 5), 4 circles to the outside of the stack and then moves back toward the foul line. 3 decoys screening for 5, lets 4 go to the outside, and then pops quickly to the wing to receive the inbound pass. As soon as 3 has received the ball, 2 moves up the lane line to set the screen for 5, who is cutting off 2's screen. 3 can look to make a direct pass on the cut or wait until 5 settles in the post. After he inbounds the ball, 1 moves quickly to the three-point line on the opposite side of the floor to take his defender out of the key area. After screening for 5, 2 moves to the ballside corner to take his defender away and to set up a potential passing angle to the post. After 5 has settled in the post, 3 reads how 5 is being defended and makes the correct pass. If 5's defender is behind, on the low side, or in front, 3 can make the direct pass. If 5's defender is on the high side, 3 can pass the ball to the corner to 2, who has a better passing angle to the post.

Coaching Points:

- 4 must circle to the high post area so the companion play (Play #42) can be executed.

- 3 decoys the screen to lull his defender and make it easier to get open on the wing.

- 2 must move up the lane line to set the screen for 5 so 5 has more room to operate. The higher the screen can be set, the better. 5 should delay his cut to allow 2 to move up.

- 2 and 3 are set in a triangle passing formation to feed the ball to 5, who is isolated at the block.

- Sequential passing reads are 1 inbounds to 3; 3 to 5 at the post; or 3 to 2, who feeds 5 at the post.

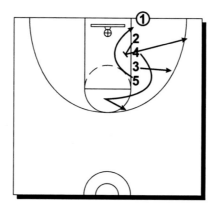

PLAY #42: STACK SET VERSUS A MAN-TO-MAN DEFENSE

Objective: High-low post feed from a "pop the stack" cut. Three passes for a shot.

Description: This play is a companion play for Play #41. From a stack set, alternating small, big (2, 4, 3, 5), this play begins the same way Play #41 did. 4 circles to the outside of the stack and 3 pops to the wing. As 3 receives the inbound pass on the wing, 1 cuts to the opposite side of the floor, and 2 again screens up for 5, who cuts off 2's screen to the block (Diagram 42a). In this play, instead of 2 moving to the ballside corner after screening, he waits for the ball to be swung to 4. 4 pops out from the high post to receive the ball from 3. As 3 passes the ball to 4, 2 screens back down on 5's defender, allowing 5 to curl over the top of the screen and receive the high-low pass from 4 (Diagram 42b).

Coaching Points:

- As 3 receives the ball, he can still look at 5 for an easy pass opportunity that could lead to a shot.

- 4 curls to the outside of the stack, toward the foul line, and then pops quickly out to the top of the circle to receive the pass from 3.

- 2 is the key person in this play. He must set two solid screens: the first one to allow 5 to make a basket cut, and the second one going back on 5, who pops the stack and curls quickly and strongly over the top of 2 into the middle of the key, holding his ground and looking for the high-low pass from 4.

- Sequential passing reads are 1 to 3 on the wing, 3 looks for 5 and then reverses the ball to 4, 4 waits for 5 to pop the stack and passes from the high post to the low post in the middle of the key.

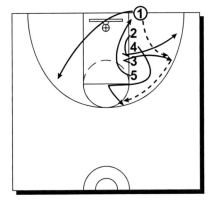

Diagram 42a

Diagram 42b

PLAY #43: STACK SET VERSUS A MAN-TO-MAN OR ZONE DEFENSE

Objective: Shooter coming off a double-screen and then little screening for big. One pass for a shot.

Description: From a stack set lined up 2, 4, 3 (shooter), and 5 (post), 3 cuts toward the basket, then curls around 2 and 4 to the corner and spots up for a shot. After 3 has curled off, 4 moves quickly to the top of the circle to clear the key area. Then 2 steps up and into the key to set a screen for 5. After screening for 5, 2 rolls back toward the ball.

Coaching Points:

- 3 can precede the original cut by moving slightly to the outside of the stack and then cutting off 4 and 2 toward the corner.

- 4 screens briefly before clearing to the top of the circle.

- 2 steps into the key to screen for 3 (so that more room is created for 3's curl to the corner) and to prepare for the next screen.

- 5 V-cuts to the outside and then cuts hard off of 2's screen.

- 2 attempts to set the screen for 5 as high as possible and at an angle that gives 5 space to get open on the far side of the basket and gives 2 room to roll back to the ball.

- 2, 5, or 4 can become the safety outlets by moving out to the perimeter after their original cuts.

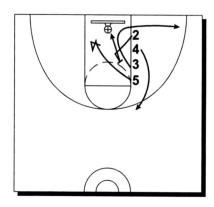

PLAY #44: STACK SET VERSUS A MAN-TO-MAN DEFENSE

Objective: Two delayed, little-to-big screens. One pass for a shot.

Description: From a stack set lined up 2 (shooter), 4, 3, 5, player 4 begins the movement by popping out to the corner and calling for the ball. 3 and 5 hold their positions as 2 steps out and sets a back screen for 4, who cuts hard toward the basket. After screening for 4, 2 pops to the corner and spots up for a shot. After 4 has cleared the nearside block, 3 sets a screen for 5, who cuts down the lane directly toward the ball.

Coaching Points:

- The further 4 pops to the corner, the more room 2 has to set the screen and 4 has to get open.

- 4 must make the first move to the corner as the ball is being handed to 1 to give the delayed part of the play enough time.

- 2 should set the screen as far out as possible to give 4 more room to get open.

- The better the screen that 2 sets, the more likely he is to be open as he pops to the corner.

- 5 decoys as if he is not in the play and then cuts off 3's delayed screen.

- Sequential passing reads are 4, 2, 5.

- 3 can move to any open area on the perimeter to become the safety outlet.

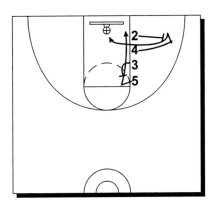

PLAY #45: STACK SET VERSUS A MAN-TO-MAN DEFENSE

Objective: Clear out for a little-to-big screen. One pass for a shot.

Description: From a stack set, the players line up 5, 4, 2 (smallest guard), and 3. As soon as the inbounder touches the ball, 4 pops to the corner and calls for the ball, and 3 clears to the far corner. 5 steps up slightly and screens for 2 cutting down the key. After screening, 5 clears to the perimeter at the top of the circle (Diagram 45a), thereby leaving the whole floor for 2 and 4. 2 continues his curl around to the outside and sets a back screen for 4, who makes a basket cut. After screening for 4, 2 pops to the corner and spots up for a shot (Diagram 45b).

Coaching Points:

- This play is similar to Play #44 except that it clears the whole key area for the back screen from 2 to 4.

- 4 must move quickly to the outside.

- 3 has to cut hard and target the ball to draw the defender with him.

- 2 cuts hard to the inside and then continues the curl immediately toward the back screen for 4.

- 5 only has to get quick contact with 2 as he cuts and then must clear to the top of the circle.

- Sequential passing reads are 4, 2, 4, 2.

- 5, 3, and 2 need to be ready to reposition to become safety outlets.

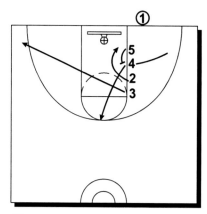

Diagram 45a

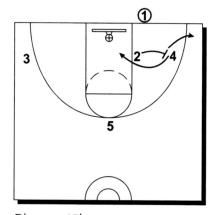

Diagram 45b

4

Random Sets

PLAY #46: RANDOM SET VERSUS A ZONE DEFENSE

Objective: Cut four players to the baseline against a zone with three defenders on the baseline. Look for a shot from one pass on a quick post or a defensive error on the cuts.

Description: From a random set, 5 starts at the ballside block, 2 is one step inside 5, 3 is one step above the ballside elbow, and 4 is at the opposite elbow. 4 begins with a move toward 3's defender and then slices down the middle of the key. 3 cuts behind 4 to the opposite corner and spots up for a shot. As 3 and 4 are cutting, 2 pops to the ballside corner with help from 5, who screens the baseline of the zone. 1 looks for any area at the base of the zone that is not covered correctly to find a player who can make the pass. If the ball is passed to 2, his first look is directly to 5 at the post.

Coaching Points:

- 3 and 4 have a good chance to be open on their cuts if 2 and 5 both have two defenders on them.

- 2 delays slightly before cutting to the ballside corner.

- If the ball goes to the corner, 5 needs to quickly pin his defender at the block and look for a direct pass from 2.

- After inbounding the ball, 1 must move quickly to defensive balance, since all four teammates are on the baseline.

- Sequential passing reads are 2 to 5.

- 3 needs to be ready to reposition himself to become the safety outlet.

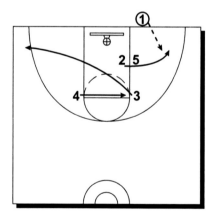

PLAY #47: RANDOM SET VERSUS A ZONE

Objective: Take advantage of the feeder-slice cut to get a shot against a zone. Three passes for a shot.

Description: This play is a companion play to Play #46. The players line up in the same positions: 2 stacked inside of 5, 3 one step above the ballside elbow, and 4 at the opposite elbow. 4 begins by moving toward 3's defender. 3 cuts behind 4 toward the opposite corner and spots up, looking for a direct pass if he's not covered. 2 pops out to the corner and receives the ball from 1. After inbounding the ball, 1 quickly clears to the top of the circle toward the area where 4 is waiting. As 2 catches the ball, 5 steps out to the feeder spot, about six feet off the key and one step off the baseline. 2 passes to 5 at the feeder spot and 4 immediately makes a slice cut down the middle of the key, looking for a direct pass from 5.

Coaching Points:

• 3 tries to drag the last defender on the baseline of the zone as far out with him as possible.

• After passing, 1 moves up toward 4 to hold 4's defender.

• As the ball is inbounded to 2, 5 pops quickly to the feeder spot, with his back toward the baseline as he receives the ball.

• 4 slices quickly down the key in the gap created by the middle defender moving out to cover 5.

• The quicker 5 can get the ball out of his hands to 4, the better the play will work.

• Sequential passing reads are 1 to 2 to 5 to 4.

PLAY #48: BOX SET VERSUS A ZONE DEFENSE

Objective: Screen the backside of the baseline in the zone, and then throw a skip pass back to the inbounder. Two passes for a shot.

Description: Players begin in a box set with the inbounder (1) being a good shooter. 5 starts on the opposite-side block, 3 on the opposite-side elbow, 4 at the ballside block, and 2 at the ballside elbow. 5 begins by stepping toward the ball to receive a direct pass if he beats his defender, or to be able to pin his defender if his cut is stopped. 2 pops out to the wing on the ballside as far as necessary to receive the inbound pass and put himself in a position to try to draw the baseline defender to him. After inbounding the ball, 1 cuts quickly to the opposite corner. 3 and 5 screen the two closest remaining defenders and 2 throws the skip pass to 1 for the shot.

Coaching Points:

- If necessary, both 5 and 3 can step toward the ball to get their defenders to deny the cut and be on the inside of them.

- 2 has to be able to physically make the skip pass or you can put another player in that position.

- If 2 can receive the ball in a location to draw the baseline defender, 5's screen will be more effective.

- 5 and 3 attempt to completely seal off the backside of the zone with their screens.

- 5 or 3 can slip the screen and cut toward 2 if their defender cheats and goes too early toward 1 in the corner.

- Sequential passing reads are 1 to 2 to 1.

- 3 and 4 need to be ready to reposition themselves to become safety outlets.

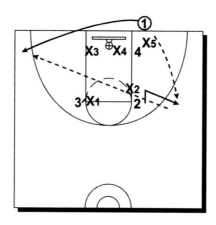

PLAY #49: RANDOM SET VERSUS A ZONE DEFENSE

Objective: Place four offensive players on the baseline against three defenders. One pass for a shot.

Description: From a random set, 4 and 5 line up to attract the two backside defenders of the base of the zone (X3 and X4). 2 and 3 stack at the foul line, with 2 on top. 3 makes the initial cut by moving to the ballside corner and attracting the last of the three baseline defenders (X5). 2 delays slightly while the three baseline defenders get matched up, and then cuts very quickly to the opposite corner. 5 screens the backside baseline defender to make the pass from 1 possible.

Coaching Points:

- 5 should take a step toward the ball to either beat his defender and receive a pass, or make his defender get on the inside of him to stop the cut, therefore making it easier to set the screen for 2.

- 2 has to delay just long enough to make sure that 5's defender is on the inside of him. 2 then moves quickly and sets up in a catch- shoot position.

- If 5's defender moves to the outside too quickly to cover 2, then 1 should be alert to 5 slipping the screen and cutting toward the ball.

- Sequential passing reads are 1 to 2.

- 3 and 4 need to be ready to reposition themselves to become safety outlets.

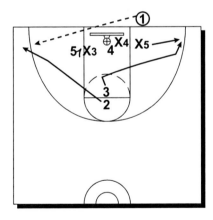

PLAY #50: RANDOM SET VERSUS A ZONE DEFENSE

Objective: Take advantage of the baseline defenders in the zone shifting after the ball has been inbounded. Three passes for a shot.

Description: From a random set, 5 lines up on the ballside elbow, 3 is one step inside 5, and 4 and 2 are stacked at the ballside block with 2 on top. 2, who is stacked with 4, pops quickly to the corner to receive the inbound pass. 3 starts in the middle of the key and sets a screen for 5, who starts at the ballside elbow. 5 cuts to the opposite block and targets the ball. After 2 receives the pass, 3 steps off the screen he set for 5 to the ballside wing to catch the pass from 2. As 3 catches the ball, the three baseline defenders should be occupied by 5, 4, and 2. 1 delays until the ball is caught by 3, then splits the gap between 4 and 2 and looks for the return pass for a shot.

Coaching Points:

- As 3 catches the pass from 2, he must look at the three baseline defenders to see if they are matched up. If the defense has not shifted correctly and 2, 4, or 5 is open, he can make the direct pass to any of them.

- If 2 and 4 are closely guarded, 3 should anticipate 1 being open in the gap.

- If 4's defender cheats out to cover 1, then 4 should be open.

- If 5's defender moves to cover 4, then 5 should be open.

- Sequential passing reads are 3 to 2 to 1.

- 5 and 2 need to be ready to reposition themselves to become safety outlets.

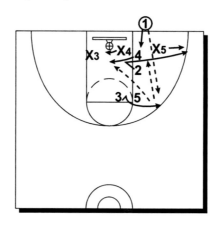

PLAY #51: RANDOM SET VERSUS A ZONE DEFENSE

Objective: Isolate two players against a specific defender in the zone. Screen and roll from the baseline. One or two passes for a shot.

Description: Players start in a random set, overloading the ballside. 4 is at the ballside block, 2 is on the three-point line, and 3 splits the middle of those two players. 5 is on the opposite-side elbow. This alignment could cause match-up problems for the baseline defenders in the zone without doing anything else. 2 initiates the play by curling under 3's screen and moving all the way to the top of the circle. To clear out the baseline, 4 pops out to the gap in the zone between the top and bottom defenders and targets the ball. After screening, 3 pops to the three-point line in the ballside corner and receives the inbound pass. As soon as 3 catches the ball, 1 steps right inbounds and sets a ball screen on the baseline side of 3's defender. 3 uses the screen and drives to the baseline side of 1, who immediately rolls over the top. 3 is looking for the shot or the drop pass to 1 on the roll, to 4 in the gap, or to 5, who delays and then slides down on the backside of the zone as 3 drives.

Coaching Points:

- Players need to know how to locate and occupy the gaps in the zone (4).

- This play can be designed to have a guard screen for a big player or vice versa.

- 5 delays and occupies the top defender until 3 starts his drive, then 5 slides down to the block on the opposite side in case the baseline of the zone shifts to help on the drive.

- Sequential passing reads are 1 to 2.

- 2 or 4 can be the safety outlets.

PLAY #52: RANDOM SET VERSUS A ZONE

Objective: Ball screen the baseline of the zone and pop out for a three-point shot. Two passes for a shot.

Description: This play is a companion play for Play #51. The players line up in the same positions they did in Play #51 and initiate the movement the same way. 2 curls under a screen by 3 and moves to the top of the circle. 4 steps into the gap in the wing of the zone. 3 pops to the three-point line after screening for 2 and receives the inbound pass from 1. 1 immediately steps in and sets a soft screen on 3's defender from the baseline side, allowing that defender to stay with 3. 3 drives toward the baseline using the screen. In this play, after screening, 1 pops back out to the three-point line for the return pass from 3. If 4 is occupying the top defender on the ballside and 3's defender stays with 3, then 1 should be wide open for the three-point shot.

Coaching Points:

- 4 needs to move high enough in the gap of the zone to make the top defender (X2) on that side cover him.

- 1 sets a soft screen that will not stop X5 from staying with 3 on the drive.

- As X5 stays with 3 and X2 is locked in with 4, no one is left to cover 1 as he pops out to the three-point line.

- Sequential passing reads are 1 to 3 to 1.

- 2 or 4 can be safety outlets.

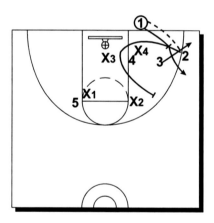

PLAY #53: RANDOM SET VERSUS A ZONE DEFENSE

Objective: Use the skip pass and a screen to attack the baseline of the zone defense. Two or three passes for a shot.

Description: Players line up across the baseline with the shooters in the corners and the posts on the blocks. 1 inbounds the ball to either corner (3 in Diagram 53a) and then quickly goes to the top of the circle for defensive balance. 1 favors the side away from the direction he passed to occupy the top defender (X1) on the side where the ball is going to be skipped. As 3 receives the inbound pass, the offense allows the three baseline defenders (X3, X4, X5) to shift and cover everyone but 3's partner (2) in the opposite corner. 3 skip passes the ball to 2 in the opposite corner (Diagram 53a). As 2 receives the ball, he looks for an open shot. On the flight time of the skip pass, 4 sets a cross screen for 5. 4 runs past X3 and screens the second defender (X4). X3 will naturally follow the skip pass to the corner and the screen on X4 will create a huge gap where 5 can get open to receive the pass from 2. As 5 comes open off 4's screen, 2 should pass him the ball for the easy shot (Diagram 53b).

Coaching Points:

- If 2 reads the screen correctly and 4 has already set the screen by the time 2 catches the ball, 2 should pass the ball quickly.

- The shorter the time that the ball is in 2's hands, the better the play will work.

- 4 must set the cross screen while the skip pass is in the air.

- Posts should identify the middle player of the three baseline defenders as their target.

- If a defender from the top of the zone drops to help on the baseline, 1 should be open for a pass and shot.

- Sequential passing reads for 1 are 2 or 3 in the corner, and 4 or 5 if their defenders move out to cover the corners.

Diagram 53a

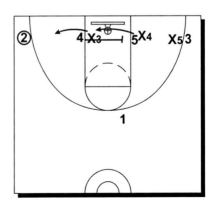

Diagram 53b

5

Lob Plays

PLAY #54: RANDOM-SET LOB PLAY VERSUS A ZONE

Objective: Get a quick shot on a lob against the baseline defenders in the zone. One pass for a shot.

Description: 5 lines up on the opposite block, 2 in the middle of the key, and 3 on the ballside block. 4 starts at the ballside elbow and begins walking before the ball is handed to the inbounder. 2 and 3 each make a move toward the outside of their original positions to occupy their defenders and make them move with them, thereby opening up the gap in the zone for 4. As soon as the referee hands the ball to 1, he throws a lob up near the basket for 4, who anticipates and is already in the air to receive it. Most defenders are used to most inbound plays beginning a second or two after the ball has been handed to the inbounder.

Coaching Points:

- As 2 and 3 widen to the outside of their original positions, they both target the ball low with their hands to get their defenders to not only widen the gap, but also to bend down to cover a low inbound pass.

- 1 and 4 need to practice the timing of the approach, jump, and pass so it is quick and accurate.

- By having 1 lob the ball as soon as it touches his hands, you will often catch the defense unprepared.

- If either 2 or 3's defender leaves him to help on the lob, he should widen more and call for the ball.

- Sequential passing reads are 4 on the lob, 2 or 3 if their defenders help, and 2, 3, or 5 as a safety outlet.

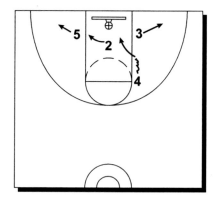

PLAY #55: RANDOM-SET LOB PLAY VERSUS MAN-TO-MAN OR ZONE DEFENSE

Objective: Get a quick shot from a lob pass against the baseline defenders in either a zone or a man defense. One pass for a shot.

Description: This play can be a companion play for Play #54. The three offensive players (5, 3, 2) line up in the same positions described for Play #54. 4 starts on the ballside elbow and begins walking toward the ball before the ball is handed to the inbounder. As the ball is handed to the inbounder, 3 and 5 widen their positions and 2 moves toward 4's defender and sets a brief screen. 4 comes off the screen and into the gap that 2 has vacated. 4 looks for the quick lob to the rim to catch and shoot before landing back on the court. 2 continues moving from the screen and cuts quickly to the three-point line, looking for a pass and shot.

Coaching Points:

- Against a man defense, it will be easy for 2 to see whom to screen. Against a zone defense, 2 will attempt to drag his middle defender out of position or screen the middle defender as 2 moves to the outside of the key area.

- The timing between 1 and 4 is critical and needs to be practiced so that the lob and jump are in sequence.

- 2, 3, or 5 can become safety outlets.

- Sequential passing reads are 4 on the lob, 2 in the corner, and then safety outlet.

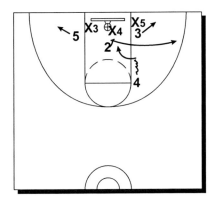

PLAY #56: RANDOM-SET LOB VERSUS A MAN-TO-MAN DEFENSE

Objective: Get a shot by lobbing the ball against a tight man-to-man defense. Two passes for a shot.

Description: From a random set, with 3 inbounding the ball, 5 aligns himself in the middle of the key, 1 is at the opposite elbow, 4 at the foul line, and 2 in the ballside corner. 5 initiates the play by screening up for 1 and then fading to the corner opposite the ball. A good leaper (3) inbounds the ball to 2 in the corner. As the ball is being inbounded, 1 doesn't use 5's screen but instead uses the screen set by 4 to cut to the ballside wing. 2 passes the ball to 1 on the wing. 3 steps inbounds and moves as if he were going to set a back screen for 2. As 1 catches the ball, he reverses direction and takes one dribble back toward the top of the key. 3 quickly changes direction at the same time and accelerates quickly back to the basket, looking for the lob to the rim from 1.

Coaching Points:

• The inbounder should be a player who can jump, so they can be in the spot to catch the lob.

• 5 must clear the key area to open it up for 3's back cut.

• 1 and 3 need to practice the timing of the catch, dribble, and pass to make it fluid.

• Sequential passing reads are 3 to 2 to 1 to 3.

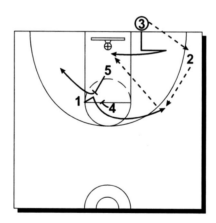

PLAY #57: RANDOM-SET LOB VERSUS A MAN-TO-MAN DEFENSE

Objective: Get a quick shot from a little to big, back pick, and a lob. One pass for a shot.

Description: Place your best jumper where 5 lines up on the nearside block. Place the person with the smallest defender in the middle of the key where 2 is located. 3 starts on the opposite block and 4 at the ballside elbow. 3 initiates the movement by cutting hard across the key, directly toward the ball, and verbally calling for the ball. 2 moves at the same time and walks up to set a back screen on 5's defender. 5 delays slightly as 3 is making his cut, then 5 targets the ball with his hands, peels back over the top with a quick change of direction, and jumps and looks for the ball at the rim for a catch and shoot. 4 moves to the ballside wing to clear out the basket area of any defensive help and to serve as a safety outlet.

Coaching Points:

- As 3 cuts across the key toward the ball, he should yell for the pass and 1 should ball fake toward him.

- 2 sets a "walking screen," where he looks more like he is cutting toward the ball than screening for 5. This movement will decoy 2's defender, making him less aware of the back screen.

- If the defenders for 2 and 5 switch, the lob opportunity should still exist—1 just throws the ball over the top to 5.

- Sequential passing reads for 1 are ball fake to 3, lob over the top to 5, and 4 as the safety outlet.

PLAY #58: BOX-SET LOB VERSUS A MAN-TO-MAN DEFENSE

Objective: Get a quick shot against a man defense with a little-to-big screen and a lob. One pass for a shot.

Description: From a box set, 3 lines up on the opposite block, 5 on the ballside block, 2 at the opposite elbow, and 4 at the ballside elbow. 3 initiates the movement by cutting across the key, going off the low side of a screen set by 5, and spotting up at the three-point line in the corner. As 3 is moving off 5's screen, 2 moves diagonally to set a screen on 5's defender. 5 sets the first screen for 3, cutting off the low side, and then quickly reverses direction and curls off of 2's screen. 5 then jumps and looks for the lob pass at the rim or the front of the basket.

Coaching Points:

- 3 must cut on the low side of the screen to get 5's defender lower to screen, and to give 5 more open space in front of the basket to receive the lob.

- 1 looks and ball fakes to 3 to get the defenders to move further out of position.

- If 2's defender switches onto 5, 1 should still look to throw the lob on the mismatch.

- 4 becomes the safety outlet.

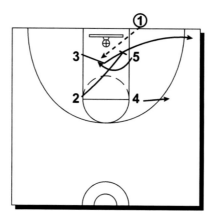

PLAY #59: STRAIGHT-LINE-SET LOB PLAY VERSUS A ZONE

Objective: Get a quick shot on a lob versus the baseline defenders in a zone. One pass for a shot.

Description: All four offensive players line up from elbow to elbow. 2 and 3 line up outside and 4 and 5 line up inside. 2 and 3 initiate the play by moving down the lane lines and then curling under the baseline of the defense out to the opposite corners. 4 and 5 delay slightly until 2 and 3 are down on the baseline, allowing the baseline of the zone to move down with the cutters. While the baseline defenders are in the low position, 4 sets a back screen on the middle defender and 5 follows directly behind, looking for the lob over the top of the middle defender. 5 should anticipate the lob and be ready to catch the ball directly above his head, not near the rim.

Coaching Points:

- 2 and 3 need to cut hard and call for the ball to make themselves active targets so the baseline of the zone must honor their cuts.

- 4 moves first. As soon as he sees the middle defender on the base of the zone sink toward the baseline, he sets the screen.

- 5 needs to move in quickly behind 4 and look for the pass to come over the top of the defender and 4. 5 needs to catch the ball in the air at its highest point.

- If the lob is not there, 4 and 5 should split the gaps on either side of the middle defender. Then, with four offensive players on the baseline, 1 needs to find the easiest entry pass.

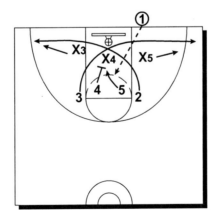

PLAY #60: BOX-SET DELAYED LOB VERSUS A MAN-TO-MAN DEFENSE

Objective: Get a shot from a little-to-big back pick on the wing with the court opened up. Three passes for a shot.

Description: Players set up in a box set with your best jumper (5) at the ballside elbow, 3 on the block opposite, 4 on the ballside block, and 2 on the opposite elbow. 4 pops quickly to the corner and 3 cuts quickly to the ballside block. 5 pops out to the ballside wing and looks for a direct pass from 1. The ball can go from 4 to 5 if necessary. As soon as 5 catches the ball, 1 circles in and moves toward 5 to get a short pass or a handoff back from 5. As soon as 5 hands the ball back to 1, 3 moves out to set a decoy screen for 4 in order to clear the basket area, and 2 moves to the ballside elbow or higher to set a back screen for 5. 5 cuts hard over the top of 2's back screen and looks for the over-the-top lob from 1.

Coaching Points:

- If the ball cannot be directly inbounded to 5, it can go to 4 first and then 4 passes to 5.

- As 5 hands the ball back to 1, 3 must move out to 4 to set an imaginary screen for 4 to clear the key of any defenders.

- As 1 receives the ball back from 5, he looks like he is going to drive to get his defender down and then throws a pass to the rim for 5 coming off 2's screen.

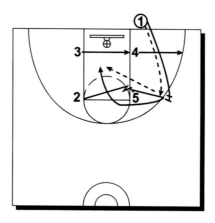

PLAY #61: TIP PASS BACK TO INBOUNDER VERSUS MAN OR ZONE

Objective: Get a quick shot by taking advantage of the player defending the inbounder. Two passes for a shot.

Description: Three players line up across the baseline with 2 on the opposite block, a big player who can jump (4) on the nearside block, and a shooter (3) in the nearside corner. The other post player (5) lines up in the middle of the foul line. Against a zone defense, 5 tries to occupy both players. Against man-to–man, 5 opens the key area. 4 aligns himself in a direct line with the ball and as close as possible to the baseline to force the defender to the baseline side. Before the ball is passed inbounds, 2 pops quickly to the three-point line to clear the lane. 1 inbounds the ball to 4 by throwing a high lob pass over the top of his defender. As the ball comes to 4, he jumps and tips it directly back to 1, who is cutting to the basket, ready to catch and shoot the ball.

Coaching Points:

- The player defending 1 will usually turn and look at the lob pass as it approaches 4. As soon as he takes his eye off of 1, 1 should cut directly to the basket and into open space to catch the return tip.

- 4 needs to line up as close to the baseline as possible, but not so close that his defender can play on the side or behind him.

- 4 should not catch the ball, but simply tip it directly toward the open spot near the rim.

- Sequential passing reads are 1 to 4 to 1.

- 2, 3, or 5 can become safety outlets.

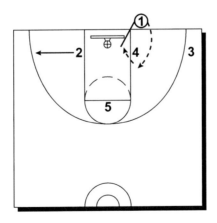

6

Bunch and Random Sets

PLAY #62: BUNCH SET VERSUS MAN DEFENSE

Objective: Set two simultaneous, big-to-little screens and read the defenders of the screeners. One pass for a shot.

Description: Players align in a diamond formation with 5 in the middle of the key, setting a screen for 2, and 4 on the nearside lane, setting a screen for 3. The screeners move first while 2 and 3 set their defenders up by targeting the ball with their hands where they stand. 5 and 4 both move toward the person they are screening for and pivot to make contact with their backs. By screening with their backs, 4 and 5 can keep vision of their defenders and also the basketball. 2 must cut hard and quick all the way through the key and 3 should cut off the screen all the way to the corner.

Coaching Points:

- 4 and 5 must complete their pivots and face the ball before they get contact. They let contact come to them.

- 2 and 3 must set up their defenders and rub off the screens tightly to force contact with 4 and 5.

- After the cutters have cleared the screens, 4 and 5 read their defenders. If the defenders stay with them, the cutter should be open. If the defenders move to help with the cutter, 4 or 5 slips the screen toward the basket.

- The better the screens 4 and 5 set, the more likely it is that they will be open.

- Any of the four players can become a safety outlet.

- Sequential passing reads are 2, 3, 5, 4.

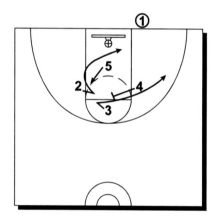

PLAY #63: BUNCH SET VERSUS MAN DEFENSE

Objective: Three cutters toward the ball, one after another. One pass for a shot.

Description: Players begin in a line across the foul line with 3 being closest to the ball, followed by 4, 5, and 2. 3 initiates the movement by screening for 4, who moves directly toward the ball. If 4 doesn't get an immediate pass, he cuts out toward the corner to clear the key. 3 then moves immediately down the line and screens for 5, who cuts for the basket and curls out to the wing if he doesn't receive an immediate pass. 3 sets the last screen for 2, who follows 5 toward the basket and then can move to any open area on the ballside. After setting the last screen, 3 fades to the opposite corner.

Coaching Points:

- 3 sets the screens with about a one-second count between each one.

- The cutters should not clog the key area if they are not immediately open.

- 3 fades quickly to the opposite corner after setting the last screen, in case his defender has moved to help on any of the three cutters.

- Sequential passing reads are 4, 5, 2, 3.

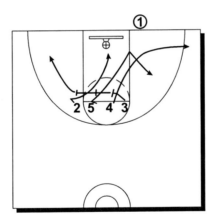

PLAY #64: BUNCH SET VERSUS MAN DEFENSE

Objective: Two big-screening-little cuts and then posts roll. One or two passes for a shot.

Description: From a bunch set, 4 and 5 line up right inside the elbows and 2 and 3 line up one step above and outside of the elbows. 2 cuts off 5's screen to the opposite corner outside the three-point line. 3 cuts off 4's screen to the ballside corner and spots up on the three-point line. Both 2 and 3 look for a direct pass as soon as they come off the first screen, and before they cut to the corners. After screening, both 4 and 5 roll directly down the side of the key on their respective sides.

Coaching Points:

- 2 and 3 can precede the cuts off the screen with a V-cut in the opposite direction. They can cut on either side of the screener.

- As soon as 2 and 3 clear the screens, they target the ball with their hands and look for a direct pass before moving to the corners.

- 4 and 5 set screens at an angle to give their cutters the best chance to get open quickly.

- 4 and 5 read the V-cut to see which direction the cutter is going to take and at which angle they should set the screen.

- 4 and 5 set solid screens and delay slightly before rolling down their respective lane lines.

- 2 and 3 can look to the post on their side if they receive the ball and do not have a shot.

- Sequential passing reads are 2, 3, 4, 5.

- Any of the four players can reposition himself to become a safety outlet.

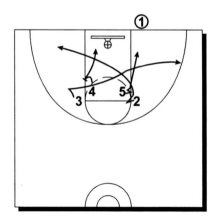

PLAY #65: BUNCH SET VERSUS A MAN-TO-MAN DEFENSE

Objective: Big-to-little cross screens, post-to-post screen and roll. One pass for a shot.

Description: From a bunch set, 2 and 3 stack inside the opposite elbow and 4 and 5 stack on the ballside elbow. 2 and 3 cross and cut off the double screen set by 4 and 5. 3 starts on top of the stack and cuts under the double screen, and 2 starts on the bottom of the stack and cuts over the top of the double screen. 3 cuts for the ballside corner and 2 cuts for the ballside wing. After 2 and 3 have cut past the screen, 5 screens up for 4, who cuts to the opposite side of the basket. 5 then rolls down the lane directly toward the ball.

Coaching Points:

• 2 and 3 V-cut in, away from the direction they want to cut past the double screen.

• 3 begins looking for a direct pass immediately after clearing the screen on the way to the corner.

• 5 lets the cutters clear the screen before setting a screen for 4 and then rolling quickly to the basket.

• If either defender on 4 or 5 helps with the cutters, one of the posts should break open.

• Sequential passing reads are 3, 4, 5.

• Any of the four players can reposition themselves to become a safety outlet.

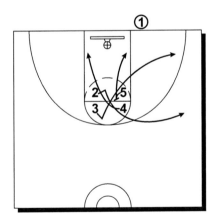

PLAY #66: BUNCH SET VERSUS A MAN-TO-MAN DEFENSE

Objective: Weave cuts, big screening little, and then post-to-post screen and roll. One or two passes for a shot.

Description: All four players line up across the foul line extended. 3 starts one step outside the opposite elbow, and 2 on the ballside wing. 4 starts just inside the opposite elbow and 5 just inside the ballside elbow. 2 weaves under 5 and then over 4 to the opposite wing. 3 weaves under 4 and over 5 to the ballside wing. After 2 and 3 have cleared the posts, 5 crosses the key and sets a screen for 4, who cuts directly down the lane toward the ball. 5 rolls off the screen and cuts to the opposite side of the basket.

Coaching Points:

- 2 and 3 must cut hard and quickly around the posts and call for the ball as they clear to the wings.

- 5 sets a screen at an angle to get 4 open on a direct cut toward the ball.

- 5 pivots off the screen and rolls down the lane, looking for a pass from 1.

- Sequential passing reads are 3, 4, 5.

- If 2 or 3 receives the ball on the wing and does not have an open shot, he should look to pass the ball to the post player on his side.

- Any of the four players can reposition themselves to become the safety outlet.

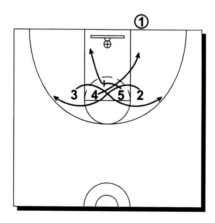

PLAY #67: RANDOM SET VERSUS A MAN-TO-MAN DEFENSE

Objective: Isolate a player of your choice at the low post. Three passes for a shot.

Description: From a random set, the player you want to isolate (5 in this case) starts at the opposite elbow. 4 and 2 start stacked at the ballside block and 3 is on the opposite block. 4 breaks out of the stack to the ballside corner to receive the inbound pass from 1, who moves to the top of the key for defensive balance. 2 cuts up and out to get open on the wing to catch the second pass from 4 (Diagram 67a). As soon as 2 catches the ball, 5 cuts down to the ballside block. When 5 arrives at the block, 2 dribbles down to the wing. As 2 dribbles, 3 cuts to the corner and 4 curls under 5 and up to the ballside elbow. 2 now has the ball on the wing, with 3 in the corner, 4 at the elbow, 5 isolated at the low post, and 1 at the top of the key (Diagram 67b). 2 simply reads how the defender is playing 5 and makes the correct pass. If 5's defender is behind or on the low side, 2 can make the pass to 5. If the defender is on the high side, 2 passes to 3 in the corner because 3 has a better passing angle. If the defender is in front of 5, 2 passes to 4 at the elbow and 4 makes a high-low entry pass to 5.

Coaching Points:

- 2 should save his dribble until 5 is positioned in the low post.

- When 4 curls around 5 toward the elbow, 5's defender may move to the high side to help on the cut. If so, 2 must read that the entry pass will come from him or 3 in the corner.

- Sequential passing reads are 1 to 4 to 2.

- Sequential passing reads from 2 are 5, 3 to 5, or 4 to 5.

- Any of the four players can reposition themselves to become safety outlets.

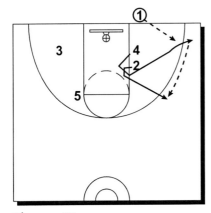

Diagram 67a

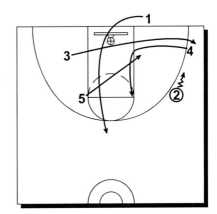

Diagram 67b

PLAY #68: RANDOM SET VERSUS A MAN-TO-MAN DEFENSE

Objective: Staggered double-screen for a shooter and little screening big on a screen-the-screener. One or two passes for a shot.

Description: From a random set, 2 starts on the opposite block and 5 on the ballside block. 4 starts in the middle of the key and 3 lines up a step outside and above the opposite elbow. 4 begins the play by stepping out to screen for 3. 5 sets a second screen for the cutting 3, who moves toward the ballside corner. As soon as 3 has cleared 5's screen, 3 looks for a direct pass and 2 steps up and screens for 5. If 5's defender helps in any way with 3's cut, 5 should be open coming off 2's screen. If 3 receives the ball in the corner and doesn't have a shot, he can wait for 5 to curl around off of 2's screen and post up on the ballside block.

Coaching Points:

- 3 must wait for the first screener (4) to come to him. 3 then cuts hard off both screens.

- 2 delays slightly until 5 has set the screen for 3, then sets a back screen on 5's defender.

- After setting the screen for 3, 5 quickly spins off the screen set by 2 and cuts to the far side of the basket.

- If the pass goes to 3, 5 should cut all the way back to the ballside block and look for an entry pass from 3.

- Sequential passing reads are 3, 5.

- 2 and 4 should be ready to reposition themselves to become safety outlets.

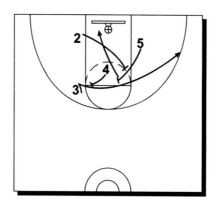

PLAY #69: RANDOM SET VERSUS A MAN-TO-MAN DEFENSE

Objective: Triple-screen for a great shooter (2). One pass for a shot.

Description: From a random set, 2 starts on the opposite block, 3 on the opposite wing, 4 inside the opposite elbow, and 5 inside the ballside elbow. 2 and 3 begin the play by 3 screening down on 2's defender and 2 circling outside of 3's screen. 2 continues curling around off 4, and then 5, on his way to any open area on the ballside of the floor. After screening, 3 fades to the corner and 4 rolls to the basket.

Coaching Points:

* 3 should be your second-best shooter. He fades to the corner after screening.

* 4 reads how 2's defender plays the first screen and moves to get solid contact before rolling to the basket.

* 5 must read how 2's defender plays the first two screens and move accordingly. If the defender is going under the screens, 5 must move lower and let 3 cut to the wing. If 2's defender is chasing over the top of the screens, then 5 moves higher to set the screen so 3 can curl toward the basket or the corner.

* Sequential passing reads are 3, 4, 2.

* 5 can move to an open area to become the safety outlet.

PLAY #70: BUNCH SET VERSUS A MAN-TO-MAN DEFENSE

Objective: Little screening big for both posts. One pass for a shot.

Description: From a bunch set, 2 starts in the middle of the key, 3 outside the opposite elbow, 4 in the middle of the foul line, and 5 at the ballside elbow. 3 is the first player to cut, moving quickly behind 4 and 5 to the ballside elbow. 2 then sets a back screen for 4, who cuts around the far side and directly toward the ball. After screening for 4, 2 moves up and screens for 5. 5 cuts off 2's screen toward the opposite side of the basket.

Coaching Points:

• 3 must cut hard and call for the ball. If he is not defended correctly, 3 could be open. But the main purpose of 3's cut is to open up the key.

• 2 can delay slightly after 3's cut to get solid contact on 4's defender.

• 4 acts as if he is going to screen for 3, then cuts off the backside of 2's screen and curls toward the ball.

• Before cutting, 5 delays and waits until 4 comes off of 2's screen and 2 gets position established on 5's defender.

• Sequential passing reads are 3, 4, 5.

• 2 or 3 can reposition themselves to become the safety outlet.

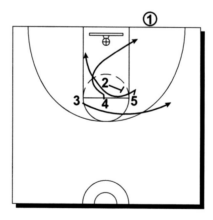

PLAY #71: BUNCH SET VERSUS A MAN-TO-MAN DEFENSE

Objective: Big screening little and then little screening big. One or two passes for a shot.

Description: From a bunch set, 4 starts in the center of the key, 2 on the opposite elbow, 3 at the top of the circle, and 5 at the ballside elbow. 3 initiates the play, cutting off 5's screen while 4 moves up to set a back screen on 2's defender. 2 cuts off 4's screen and sets a screen for 5. 5 cuts off 2's screen to the far side of the basket. After screening, 2 rolls toward the ball. If neither 5 nor 2 is open, the pass can go to 3 (Diagram 71b). If 3 receives the pass, then 2 moves across the key and sets a screen for 5 to come to the low post on the ballside.

Coaching Points:

- 4 and 3 can move simultaneously.

- 2 acts like he is going to cut off 4's screen toward the ball before turning to set the screen for 5.

- After 3 cuts off him, 5 holds his position and waits for 2 to establish a legal screening position.

- Sequential passing reads are 5, 2, 3.

- 4 or 3 can reposition themselves to become safety outlets.

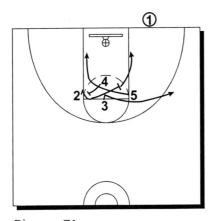

Diagram 71a

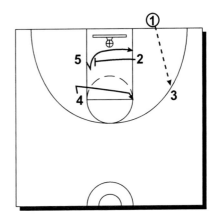

Diagram 71b

PLAY #72: BUNCH SET VERSUS MAN-TO-MAN

Objective: Little screening for both big players. One or two passes for a shot.

Description: From a bunch set, 2 lines up in the middle of the key, 4 on the opposite elbow, 3 at the top of the circle, and 5 on the ballside elbow. 3 initiates the movement by cutting hard off of a stationary screen set by 5 and moving to the ballside corner. At the same time, 2 sets a back screen on 4, and 4 cuts hard directly toward the ball. After 3 has cleared his screen, 5 cuts off 2's stationary screen to the far side of the basket.

Coaching Points:

- 2 must set two solid screens, first for 4 and then for 5.

- If 2's defender switches on either cutter, then that post player should have a mismatch.

- If 5's defender moves to help on 3's cut, then it will be difficult for that defender to not be trailing 5 when he cuts.

- 1 needs to watch how 4 and 5's defenders play the screens to give him an indication of who may be coming open.

- Sequential passing reads are 3, 4, 5.

- After setting the two screens, 2 can reposition to become the safety outlet.

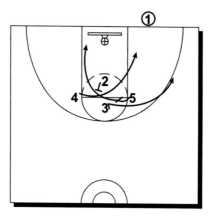

PLAY #73: RANDOM SET VERSUS A MAN-TO-MAN OR ZONE DEFENSE

Objective: Clear the key and then little screening big coming into the key. One, two, or three passes for a shot.

Description: From a bunch set, 2, 3, and 5 stack on the ballside of the key, with 2 starting on the block. 4 lines up on the opposite elbow. 2 initiates the play by curling to the inside of the stack and moving all the way back around to the ballside corner. As soon as 2 has cleared the stack, 5 cuts hard to the opposite block and 3 sets a diagonal screen for 4, who curls off the screen and splits the middle of the key or the gap in the zone (Diagram 73a). If 2 receives the ball in the corner and does not have a shot, he should look for 4 on the ballside block and 5 can flash back to the high post for a possible high-low pass to 4 (Diagram 73b).

Coaching Points:

- 2 must make an explosive cut to the inside of the stack and back to the corner to draw defensive attention from either his defender or the base of the zone. The explosive cut will first compress a zone and then extend it to cover the corner.

- 5 cuts without any screen to occupy the baseline defenders in a zone.

- 4 cuts off 3's screen and looks to rub his defender off against man-to-man defense or to fill the gap created in the baseline of a zone defense.

- If 5 sees that the pass has gone to 2 in the corner, he can move to the ballside high post to potentially make the high-low pass to 4 on the block.

- Sequential passing reads are 2, 5, 4, 2-to-4, or 2-to-5-to-4.

- After setting the screen for 4, 3 can reposition and become the safety outlet.

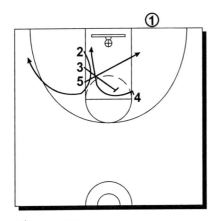

Diagram 73a

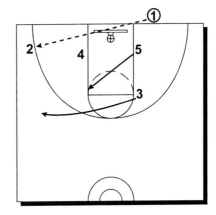

Diagram 73b

PLAY #74: BUNCH SET VERSUS A MAN-TO-MAN OR ZONE DEFENSE

Objective: Set up a high-low passing angle with a little-to-big screen. Two or three passes for a shot.

Description: From a bunch set, 2 lines up in the middle of the key, 3 on the opposite elbow, 5 at the foul line, and 4 on the ballside elbow. 3 and 4 cut simultaneously. 3 cuts across the foul line to the ballside wing. 4 cuts down through the key to the opposite corner. 5 sets a down screen for 2 and then moves his defender as far down in the key as possible. 2 comes up off 5's screen and looks to receive the inbound pass. As he receives the pass, 2 immediately looks to 5, who should have sealed his defender off and should be ready to receive the high-low pass to score (Diagram 74a). If 5's defender has moved up on top of 5, then 2 can pass to either 3 or 4, who will have a better passing angle to 5 (Diagram 74b).

Coaching Points:

- 3 and 4 cut through to the opposite side to clear the key and allow 5 to operate alone in the key.

- As 5 screens down for 2, he continues walking his defender down toward the ball, forcing his defender to stay on the low side to prevent the direct pass from 1, and getting him closer to the basket when the pass does go to 2.

- As 1 is passing the ball to 2, 2 should already be looking to see if 5 has successfully "pinned" his defender down low.

- If 2 can't make the direct pass to 5, he looks for either wing to make the entry pass.

- Sequential passing reads are 2-to-5 or 2-to-3 (or 4)-to-5.

- Any of the four players can reposition to become the safety outlet.

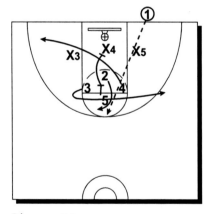

Diagram 74a

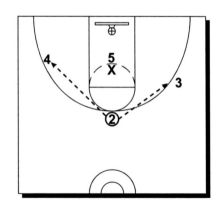

Diagram 74b

PLAY #75: BUNCH SET VERSUS A MAN-TO-MAN DEFENSE

Objective: Post isolation after a little-to-big screen or a step-out three-point shot for the inbounder. Two passes for a shot.

Description: From a bunch set, 3 lines up in the middle of the key, 4 on the opposite elbow, 2 at the top of the circle, and your best post player (5) at the nearside elbow. 3 moves up, sets a back screen on 2's defender, and then fades to the farside wing. 2 cuts off the screen and then curls to the ballside wing off a stationary screen by 5. As 2 receives the inbound pass from 1 at the wing, 1 moves quickly up the lane to set a back screen for 5. 5 cuts off the screen to the block and 1 steps out to the three-point line. 2 has the option to pass to 5 at the block or to 1 at the top of the three-point line.

Coaching Points:

- Let your best three-point shooter inbound the ball and step out off the back screen to the three-point line.

- 2 reads the screen between 1 and 5. If the defenders switch, 5 has a mismatch. If 5's defender gets caught by the screen, the defender will be trailing 5 on the cut and 5 should be immediately open. If 1's defender hedges to help on 5's cut, then 1 should be wide open for a catch-and-shoot three-pointer.

- Sequential passing reads are 1-to-2-to-5 or 1-to-2-to-1.

- 3 or 4 can reposition themselves to become safety outlets.

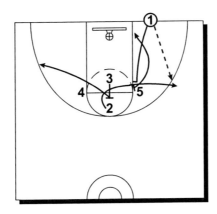

PLAY #76: BUNCH SET VERSUS A MAN-TO-MAN DEFENSE

Objective: Big screening little for the inbounder. Two or three passes for a shot.

Description: From a bunch set, 3 lines up in the middle of the key, 4 on the opposite elbow, 2 at the top of the circle, and 5 at the ballside elbow. 2 initiates the play by screening down for 3 and then immediately cutting off a stationary screen by 5 to the ballside wing. As soon as 2 receives the inbound pass, 5 moves quickly down the key to set a screen on 1's defender. 1 delays after inbounding the ball and then curls off 5's screen, looking for a return pass and shot from the corner. 5 posts up after setting the screen.

Coaching Points:

- Let your best offensive player (1 in this case) inbound the ball and receive the screen.

- 2 must cut hard off 5's screen to get himself open for the inbound pass.

- If 5 and 1's defenders switch, both have a mismatch—1 with a big defender on the perimeter, and 5 with a little defender on the block.

- Sequential passing reads are 1-to-2-to-1, 1-to-2-to-5, or 1-to-2-to-1-to-5.

- Either 3 or 4 can reposition themselves to become the safety outlet.

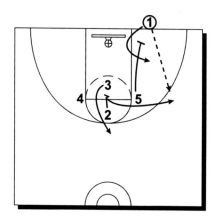

PLAY #77: BUNCH SET VERSUS A MAN-TO-MAN OR ZONE DEFENSE

Objective: Little screening big and then sliding to open areas on the baseline. One or two passes for a shot.

Description: From a bunch formation, 3 lines up in the middle of the key, your best post (5 in this case) on the opposite elbow, 4 at the top of the circle, and 2 on the ballside elbow. 3 and 4 initiate the play with 4 screening down for 3 and then slipping the screen to cut to the ballside corner. After 4 has cleared the foul line, 2 cuts across the key and sets a screen for 5. 5 cuts off the screen directly toward the ball. 2 rolls off the screen to the opposite block. If 4 receives the pass and does not have an open shot, he should look for 5 posting up on the block.

Coaching Points:

- 2 moves to screen 5 right off the back of 4.

- 5 can set his defender up for the screen by backing out a step and calling for the ball.

- Sequential passing reads are 4, 5, 2, or 1-to-4-to-5.

- 3 should be ready to reposition himself to become the safety outlet.

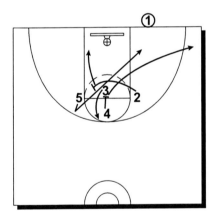

PLAY #78: RANDOM SET VERSUS A MAN-TO-MAN OR ZONE DEFENSE

Objective: Crossing action by the two guards and both posts brought back toward the ball. One pass for a shot.

Description: From a random set, 4 starts on the ballside block, 5 at the ballside elbow, 3 at the foul line, and 2 at the opposite midpost. 4 initiates the play by moving up the lane line to set a screen for 3 cutting to the ballside and then for 2 cutting to the ballside wing. As 4 moves up the lane, 5 V-cuts into the lane and then back directly toward the ball. After 2 has cleared 4's screen, 4 rolls to the basket.

Coaching Points:

- 4 must screen at the proper angle to free up both 2 and 3 as they cut to the ballside.

- 5 makes his first move into the middle of the key to freeze the middle defender of the zone, then cuts back to the ballside block, looking for a direct pass.

- As 4 rolls off the screen, he must identify the open gaps in the baseline defense.

- Sequential passing reads are 5, 3, 2, 4.

- 2 and 3 need to be ready to reposition themselves to become the safety outlets.

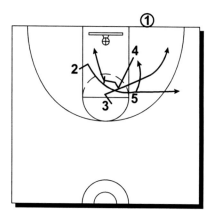

PLAY #79: BUNCH SET VERSUS A MAN-TO-MAN DEFENSE

Objective: Big screening little and then screen-the-screener, little screening big. One or two passes for a shot.

Description: From a bunch set, 4 and 5 stack on the ballside low post with 5 on the top of the stack. 3 lines up at the ballside elbow and 2 in the middle of the key, in front of the basket. 4 curls to the outside of 5, as 3 V-cuts into the key, preparing to receive the screen. 4 screens for 3, who curls around the screen and cuts directly to the ball. As 4 is screening for 3, 2 moves up and screens 4's defender. 4 cuts off the screen to the open part of the key (Diagram 79a). If neither 3 nor 4 is open to make a shot, 1 can look to lob the ball to 5 or pass to 3 in the corner, 2 on the wing, or 4 at the high post. The player who receives the pass then looks to enter the ball to 5 at the low post (Diagram 79b).

Coaching Points:

- 3 and 4 move simultaneously to initiate the play.

- 2 delays slightly, waiting for 4 to establish position for the first screen.

- Sequential passing reads are 3, 4, and then 1-to-3-to-5.

- 2 or 3 can reposition themselves to become the safety outlet.

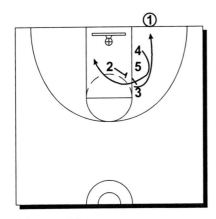

Diagram 79a

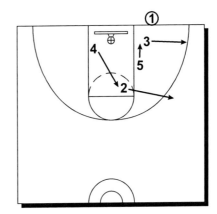

Diagram 79b

PLAY #80: BUNCH SET VERSUS A MAN-TO-MAN OR ZONE DEFENSE

Objective: Quick hitter with cutters circling through the baseline and a little-to-big screen. One or two passes for a shot.

Description: From a bunch set, 2 lines up on the ballside block, 3 one step inside the ballside elbow, 5 at the ballside elbow, and 4 one step outside the ballside elbow. 3 and 4 initiate the play by circling hard under 2 at the low post and looking for a direct pass from 1. After 3 and 4 have circled under 2, 2 moves up the lane and screens for 5, who cuts directly toward the ball (Diagram 80a). If the pass cannot be made to 3, 4, or 5, 1 can enter the ball to 3 in the corner and 3 then looks to pass to 5 in the ballside low post. The ball can also be entered from 2 on the wing or 4 at the ballside high post. (Diagram 80b).

Coaching Points:

- Against a zone, the circle cuts by 3 and 4 should widen the baseline defenders and open up the cut by 5.

- If 1 sees the baseline of the zone collapse back on 5's cut, then either 3 or 4 should be open for a shot.

- 2 needs to delay before screening up for 5.

- Sequential passing reads are 4, 3, 5, and then 1-to-3-to-5.

- 2 needs to be ready to reposition himself to become a safety outlet.

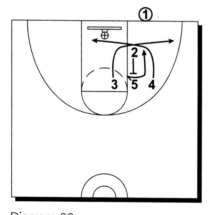
Diagram 80a

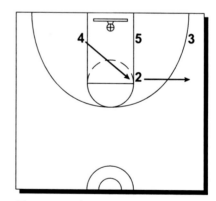
Diagram 80b

PLAY #81: RANDOM SET VERSUS A MAN-TO-MAN DEFENSE

Objective: Three quick, consecutive, little-to-big screens by the same player. One or two passes for a shot.

Description: From a random set, 5 starts one step outside the opposite block, 4 at the opposite elbow, 3 on the ballside block, and 2 one step outside the ballside block. 3 starts the play by cutting quickly to the outside of 2's screen, looking for a direct pass and shot. Before 2 sets the next screen, he looks to see if his defender has helped on 3's cut so he could slip the screen and receive a direct pass. If the ball is entered to 3, 2 screens across for 5. 5 makes a cut off the screen to the ballside low post. 2 then continues screening by moving up the lane to set a back screen for 4, who cuts down the lane.

Coaching Points:

- 1's first look is at 2's defender to see if 2 can get open by slipping the screen he set for 3. If 2 cannot get open, 1 should enter the ball to 3 and then hustle to the top of the circle for defensive balance.

- 2 sets the cross screen for 5 and immediately moves up to set the back screen for 4.

- Sequential passing reads are 2 on the slip, 3 in the corner, and then 1-to-3-to-5, or 1-to-3-to-4.

- 2 and 3 need to be ready to reposition themselves if necessary to become the safety outlets.

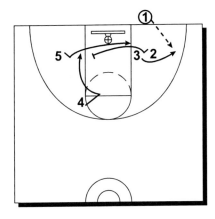

PLAY #82: BUNCH SET VERSUS A MAN-TO-MAN OR ZONE DEFENSE

Objective: Quick, high-post split, slashing play with four players ending up on the baseline. One pass for a shot.

Description: From a bunch set, 3 starts at the opposite block, 4 at the ballside elbow, 2 one step to the inside of 4, and 5 one step to the outside of 4. 3 pops quickly to the corner and spots up for a three-point shot. 2 and 5 split the post, with 2 going first and ending up on the outside. 5 V-cuts to the outside and then cuts over the top of 4, down the key to the far side of the basket. After 2 and 5 have split the post, 4 cuts directly down the lane toward the ball.

Coaching Points:

• 3 pops hard to the three-point line to open up the key and drag the outside baseline defender with him.

• Against a zone, one of the other three cutters (2, 4, or 5) should be open if the outside defender has moved out with 3.

• The cuts by 2 and 5 need to be quick and hard.

• 4 needs to identify the gaps in the defense and cut to the openings.

• Sequential passing reads are 3, 2, 5, 4.

• 2 and 3 need to be ready to reposition themselves to become the safety outlet.

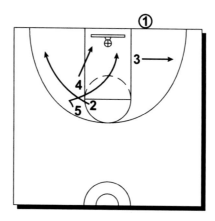

PLAY #83: RANDOM SET VERSUS A MAN-TO-MAN OR A ZONE DEFENSE. ONE OR TWO PASSES FOR A SHOT.

Objective: Spread out the defense and then a quick attack of the baseline with two big-to-little screen and rolls.

Description: From a random set, 4 starts on the opposite midpost, 3 at the foul line, 2 stacked above 3, and 5 on the ballside midpost. 4 and 5 move up simultaneously to set screens. 4 screens for 3 to get open on the opposite wing, and 5 screens for 2 to get open on the ballside wing. After 2 and 3 have cleared the screens, 4 and 5 roll off the screens and cross the key (Diagram 83a). If none of the four cutters is open for a shot, the entry pass can go to 2 or 3 in the corners and they can look for the player (4 or 5) on their side in the low post (Diagram 83b).

Coaching Points:

- The first screens can be staggered if the timing is better for your players. 4 would screen for 3 first, and then a count later, 5 would screen for 2.

- After 4 and 5 screen, instead of rolling directly toward the ball, they cross in the key.

- If the outside baseline defenders in a zone cover 2 and 3 on their cuts to the corners, one of the two post players should be open on the roll.

- Sequential passing reads are 3, 2, 4, 5, 1-to-3-to-5, or 1-to-2-to-4.

- Any of the four players needs to be ready to reposition himself to become the safety outlet.

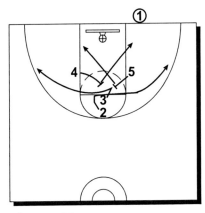

Diagram 83a

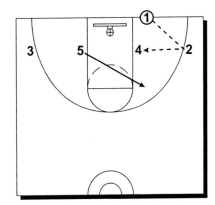

Diagram 83b

PLAY #84: RANDOM SET VERSUS MAN-TO-MAN

Objective: Quick strike with three options. One pass for a shot.

Description: From a random formation, 5 lines up on the ballside block, 3 just inside the opposite block, 2 at the top of the circle, and 4 at the near elbow. 5 initiates the movement by setting a cross screen on 3, who cuts hard to the corner, looking to catch and shoot. As soon as 3 has cleared the key, 4 slices directly toward the ball. 5 then sets a back screen for 2, who cuts to the far side of the basket.

Coaching Points:

- This play is a timing play, with 3 cutting first, followed immediately by 4, and by that time, 2 is coming off 5's screen.

- If 1 thinks 4 is going to be open, he can ball fake toward 3 to widen the defense.

- If 1 reads 5's screen and thinks 2 is going to be open, he can ball fake toward 4 to squeeze the defense.

- Sequential passing reads are 3, 4, 2.

- 2, 3, and 5 need to be ready to reposition themselves to become the safety outlet.

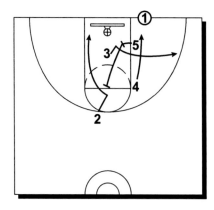

PLAY #85: BUNCH SET VERSUS A MAN-TO-MAN DEFENSE

Objective: Two little-to-big screens. One or two passes for a shot.

Description: From a bunch set, 3 lines up in the middle of the key, 2 on the ballside elbow, 4 in the middle of the foul line, and 5 on the opposite elbow. 3 initiates the movement by setting a screen for 5 to cut to the ballside wing. After 3 screens, he clears to the wing opposite. After 5 cuts, 2 screens for 4, who V-cuts and curls down the lane, looking for a pass from 5.

Coaching Points:

- 5 reads his defender and can cut over or under the screen set by 3.
- 2 must wait until 5 is receiving the ball to set the screen on 4.
- 4 has to V-cut away to allow 2 to get a good angle on his defender.
- Sequential passing reads are 5 for a shot or 1-to-5-to-4.
- 2 must be ready to reposition himself to become a safety outlet.

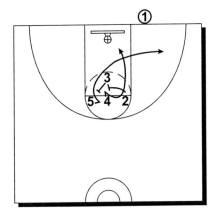

PLAY #86: BUNCH SET VERSUS A MAN-TO-MAN DEFENSE

Objective: Little-to-big screen and then double-screen for the best shooter. Two passes for a shot.

Description: From a bunch set, 2 starts on the ballside block, 5 on the opposite block, and 3 and 4 side by side at the foul line. 2 initiates the play by setting a cross screen on 5. 5 cuts hard to the ballside and receives the inbound pass from 1. As soon as 5 receives the inbound pass, 3 and 4 screen down for 2, who curls to the top, looking for a catch-shoot opportunity.

Coaching Points:

- This play is a screen-the-screener play, so if 2's defender helps on 5's cut at all, 2 should be open.

- 3 and 4 move in unison and shoulder to shoulder to set the double-screen for 2.

- If either 3 or 4's defender moves out to help on 2's cut to the top, they can slip the screen and look for a pass from 5.

- Sequential passing reads are 1-to-5-to-2 or 1-to-5-to-3 (or 4) slipping the screen.

- 3 and 4 need to be ready to reposition themselves to become safety outlets.

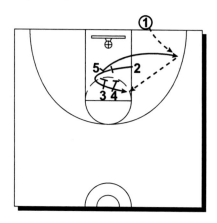

PLAY #87: RANDOM SET VERSUS A MAN-TO-MAN DEFENSE

Objective: Staggered double-screen for a lob or post-up or shooter slipping the screen. Two passes for a shot.

Description: This play is a companion play for Play #86. From a random set, 2 lines up on the ballside block, 5 on the opposite block, and 3 and 4 side by side at the foul line. 2 initiates the play by screening across for 5. At the same time, 4 is either V-cutting away from 3, then quickly cutting back toward 3's screen and off of 2's screen, looking for the lob from 5, or 4 is cutting all the way to the ballside post. After 2 sets the screen, he moves quickly to the ballside wing, looking for a catch-shoot opportunity.

Coaching Points:

- The beginning of this play is exactly like the start of Play #86, but instead of 3 and 4 screening down for 2, 3 screens for 4 and then 2 screens for 4.

- If 2's defender switches onto 4, a lob opportunity may still occur with the mismatch.

- If 2's defender hesitates at all trying to help on 4's cut, then 2 should be open on the wing.

- Sequential passing reads are 1-to-5-to-4 on the lob, 1-to-5-to-4 at the post, or 1-to-5-to-2 for the shot on the wing.

- 2 and 3 need to be ready to reposition themselves to become the safety outlet.

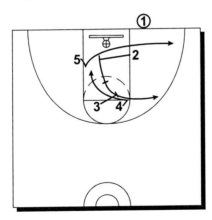

PLAY #88: BUNCH SET VERSUS A MAN-TO-MAN OR ZONE DEFENSE

Objective: Quick hitter with a shooting option for all four players. One pass for a shot.

Description: From a bunch set, 4 lines up one step below the ballside elbow, 5 is on the ballside elbow, 2 is one step below the middle of the foul line, and 3 is on the middle of the foul line. 2 cuts first, going over the top of 5's stationary screen to the ballside wing, looking for a catch-and-shoot opportunity. 4 moves right off 2's back and sets a back screen for 3, who cuts hard directly toward the outside of the key on the ballside. After screening for 3, 4 rolls to the backside of the basket. 5 waits until 4 rolls and then splits the gap created by the cuts of 3 and 4.

Coaching Points:

*   This play is a timing play, so all the screens and cuts must take place with precision.
*   2's first cut over the top of 5 must be defended or he can receive the ball.
*   The better the screen 4 sets on 3, the more likely 4 is to be open on the roll.
*   Sequential passing reads are 2, 3, 4, 5.
*   2 and 3 need to be ready to reposition themselves to become safety outlets.

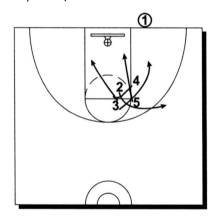

PLAY #89: BUNCH SET VERSUS A MAN-TO-MAN DEFENSE

Objective: Cutter coming toward the ball off a double-screen with little screening big. Two passes for a shot.

Description: From a bunch set, all four players are in a tight square, with 4 and 5 on the bottom and 2 and 3 on the top. 4 and 5 start the movement by crossing under, with 5 cutting toward the ballside and 4 toward the opposite side. After the ball is inbounded to 5, 2 and 3 set a double-screen for 4, who cuts either high or low around the double toward 5 (Diagram 89a). If 4 cuts under the bottom of the double, 2 and 3 can pop the stack by having the player on the top of the double (2) screen down for 3, who curls up and to the middle of the key, looking for the pass and jump shot (Diagram 89b).

Coaching Points:

- 4 and 5 cut as soon as the ball is handed to 1.
- If 5 needs a screen to get open, 4 can stay in place and set the screen before moving to the outside.
- When 4 moves outside, he must target the ball so his defender has to move out with him, setting him up for the double.
- 2 and 3 pop the stack as soon as 4 has cleared the double.
- If 4 goes under the double, then 2 screens down for 3.
- If 4 goes over the top of the double, then 3 screens up for 2, who curls under to the basket.
- Sequential passing reads are 1-to-5-to-4 and 1-to-5-to-2 (or 3) popping the stack.
- 2 and 3 need to be ready to reposition themselves to become a safety outlet.

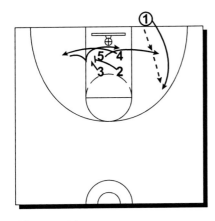

Diagram 89a

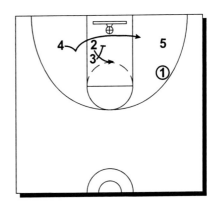

Diagram 89b

PLAY #90: RANDOM SET VERSUS A MAN-TO-MAN DEFENSE

Objective: Isolate the best shooter and the best post on the same side. Two or three passes for a shot.

Description: From a random set, the best shooter (2) starts off on the ballside block, the best post (5) on the ballside elbow, 4 on the middle of the foul line, and 3 on the opposite elbow. 3 initiates the play by weaving his way under 4 and then over 5 to the ballside wing to receive the inbound pass. After he passes the ball inbounds, 1 fills the ballside corner. As soon as 3 catches the ball, 2 sets a back screen for 5, who cuts down the lane to the low post. 2 steps out from the screen to the three-point line, looking for a catch-and-shoot opportunity. If 1 has a better passing angle from the corner, 3 can pass to 1, who can pass to 5 in the low post.

Coaching Points:

- 3 must cut hard to get open on the ballside wing or the play stalls.

- 5 waits for the screen from 2 to come to him.

- 5 can V-cut to set up the cut to the low post.

- 2 pops quickly off the screen to look for the three-point shot.

- Once 5 gets positioned on the block, he seals his defender on whatever side his defender has chosen to play him.

- If 5's defender is behind, 3 can enter the ball to the post. If the defender is on the high side, 3 passes to 1, who enters the ball from the baseline. If 5's defender is on the low side or the front, 3 can pass the ball to 2 to make the high-low entry pass.

- Sequential passing reads are 1-to-3-to-5 (or 2), 1-to-3-to-1-to-5, or 1-to-3-to-2-to-5).

- Any of the four players on the floor can reposition to become the safety outlet.

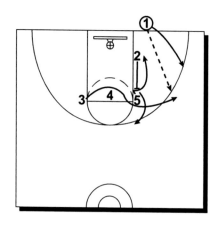

Side Out-of-Bounds Plays

In side out-of–bounds situations, the coach can be conservative and just make sure that the ball gets inbounds, or can be more aggressive and use this opportunity to try to score. Safe plays are easy to design, but you should give your team a chance to score by running a play toward the basket. If nothing else, execute cuts and screens that the defense must cover to prevent you from scoring.

PLAY #91: SIDE OUT-OF-BOUNDS VERSUS MAN-TO-MAN DEFENSE

Objective: Quick hitter by setting a big-to-little back screen for the inbounder. Two or three passes for a shot.

Description: From a double-stack set, 3 lines up on the opposite elbow, 4 steps above him, 2 starts on the ballside elbow, and 5 is two steps above him. 2 initiates the movement by setting a back screen for 5. 5 appears to be running a cut for a lob and then curls back toward a direct line between 1 and the basket. 1 inbounds the ball to 2, who is stepping out from the screen he set. As 2 catches the ball, 4 screens down for 3, who comes off the screen looking for 2 to reverse the ball to him. At the same time, 1 walks inbounds to delay slightly, V-cuts, and sprints past 5's screen, looking for the catch and lay-in. The ball can be thrown to 1 either by 2 after he ball fakes to 3, or by 3 after catching the reversal pass from 2.

Coaching Points:

• The timing of 1's cut is critical so that either 2 or 3 is ready to make the pass.

• The simplest option is for 2 to ball fake to 3 to take the defenders' eyes off the cut by 1. On the ball fake, 1 sprints off 5's screen.

• If 5's defender switches onto 1, the defense is in a mismatch situation and either 1 or 5 will have an advantage. 1 can then cut all the way to the far corner and 5 can take his defender down to the block and look for a high-low entry pass.

• Sequential passing reads are 1-to-2-to-1, 1-to-2-to-3-to-1, and 1-to-2-to-5 at the block.

• If 2 doesn't have an easy pass, he can become the safety outlet.

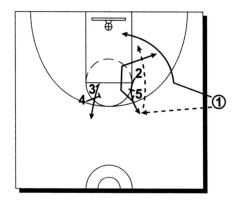

PLAY #92: SIDE OUT-OF-BOUNDS VERSUS A MAN-TO-MAN DEFENSE

Objective: A box set, with a little-to-big back screen and the best shooter (3) coming to the three-point line. Three passes for a shot.

Description: From a box set, 3 lines up on the opposite block, 5 on the opposite elbow, 2 on the ballside block, and 4 at the ballside elbow. 4 initiates the movement by V-cutting into the key, quickly reversing direction, and popping out toward the ball to receive the inbound pass. As soon as 4 catches the pass, 1 immediately follows his pass and gets a short pass or handoff back from 4. After receiving the ball back, 1 dribbles toward the far side of the court toward a stationary screen set by 5. After 5 sets the screen for 1, he immediately screens down for 3. Two things are happening simultaneously: 3 is coming up off 5's screen and 2 steps up to set a back screen for 4, who is cutting for the basket, looking for a pass or lob. 1 chooses the better of the two options (3 or 4).

Coaching Points:

- Timing is critical for this play to work. If it is easier for 1 to read the play one movement at a time, the down screen by 5 and the back screen by 2 can be slightly staggered, with 2 going first.

- 1 must be able to dribble with his head and eyes up to see the options.

- 5 can slip the screen and go to the basket, and 2 can step out from his screen, looking for a pass back and a shot from the perimeter.

- Sequential passing reads are 1-to-4-to-1-to-4 and 1-to-4-to-1-to-3.

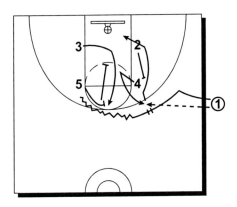

PLAY #93: SIDE OUT-OF-BOUNDS VERSUS MAN-TO-MAN DEFENSE

Objective: Single-stack set for a quick screen and roll with big screening little. Two or three passes for a shot.

Description: From a single-stack set, 2 lines up on the opposite block, 4 on the opposite elbow, and 1 is stacked under 5 at the ballside elbow. On this play, use 3 to inbound the ball so that the best ball handler (1) is dribbling the ball off 5's screen. 2 initiates the movement by cutting hard to the ballside corner. At the same time, 1 cuts up off the stack, using 5 as a stationary screener. As soon as 1 receives the ball, 3 clears to the opposite side and 5 sets a ball screen on the baseline side of 1. 1 uses the screen and turns the corner, keeping his dribble alive. 5 rolls off the screen to the open key area and 1 reads the defense to see who has come open after clearing the screen.

Coaching Points:

- 5 sets two screens. First, at the beginning of the play, he sets a screen to get 1 open at the top. Second, 5 sets a ball screen as soon as 1 has received the ball.

- 1 has three options: drive to the basket, pass to 5 on the roll, or pass to 2 in the corner.

- As 1 turns the corner off of 5's screen, 2 should already be spotted up in the corner. 1 looks to see if 2's defender leaves him to help on the drive, and if he does, 2 should be open for a three-point shot.

- Sequential passing reads are 3-to-1-to-5 or 3-to-1-to-2.

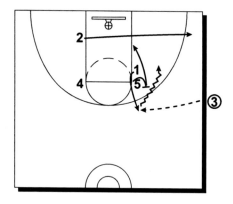

PLAY #94: SIDE OUT-OF-BOUNDS VERSUS A MAN-TO-MAN DEFENSE

Objective: Random set to isolate the point guard and the post on a quick give-and-go cut.

Description: From a random set, 2, 3, and 4 line up at the top of the circle and 5 starts at the ballside low post. 2, 3, and 4 occupy their defenders by 3 cutting toward the basket and then coming back to the top off of a double-screen set by 2 and 4. 5 starts in at the ballside block in a direct line between the ball and the basket. He calls for the ball at the block before popping out toward the ball, receiving it about 15 to 18 feet from the basket. As soon as 5 catches the ball, 1 V-cuts high and cuts low off 5 or V-cuts low and cuts over the top of 5, looking for the return pass and shot. If the return pass is not available, then 5 turns and faces the basket, looking for the drive.

Coaching Points:

- This play is a good one to run for any level of basketball.
- This play is a good option if you have an advantage in quickness or if you are trying to draw a foul on 5's defender.
- Ideally, 1 will be able to make the direct pass to 5 while he is in the low post.
- Sequential passing reads are 1 to 5 to 1.
- 2, 3, and 4 can reposition themselves and become the safety outlets.

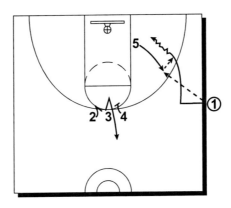

PLAY #95: SIDE OUT-OF-BOUNDS VERSUS A MAN-TO-MAN DEFENSE

Objective: Random set for a little-to-big screen-the-screener, lob, or continuation to a screen-down jumper. One pass for a shot.

Description: From a random set, 2 lines up on the opposite block, 3 on the ballside block, and 4 and 5 at the top of the circle. 4 initiates the movement by screening for 5. As 4 is screening, 3 steps out toward the ball to open up the key area, and 2 moves up to set a back screen for 4. 5 V-cuts and comes back toward the ball. After 4 has set the screen, he cuts off the screen and goes over the top of 2's back screen, heading for the basket and looking for a lob pass from 1 (Diagram 95a). If the lob is not open, then 5 screens back down for 2, who cuts to the top of the circle, looking for the three-point shot (Diagram 95b).

Coaching Points:

- Both phases of this play should happen quickly, with 2 setting the back screen for 4 and then immediately getting a screen from 5.

- The better the screen that 4 sets, the more likely he is to be open on the lob.

- The better the screen that 2 sets for 4, the more likely he is to be open for the jumper.

- Sequential passing reads are 4 for the lob and 2 for the jumper.

- 3 and 5 need to be ready to reposition themselves to become safety outlets.

Diagram 95a

Diagram 95b

PLAY #96: SIDE OUT-OF-BOUNDS VERSUS A MAN-TO-MAN DEFENSE

Objective: Random set to a quick hitter with a staggered triple-screen for the best shooter (2), followed by a little-to-big screen in the post. One or two passes for a shot.

Description: From a random set, 2 stacks below 5 on the opposite block, 3 starts on the foul line, and 4 is at the ballside elbow. 2 initiates the movement by curling around a stationary screen set by 5, then off of 3's screen, and finally off of a screen set by 4. 2 should receive the ball at the three-point line in position to shoot. As soon as 1 has inbounded the ball, he cuts hard for the basket, looking for a return pass. If 2 does not have an open shot, he dribbles down to the wing and 1 screens across for 5, who cuts to the ballside block and posts up, looking for a pass from 2.

Coaching Points:

- The screens set by 3 and 4 should be done to free up 2 at the three-point line, not further out.

- 4 and 5 should anticipate if 2 is going to shoot, and head for the offensive rebound.

- If 2 doesn't have a shot, then 4 should stay out of the key so that 1 and 5 have room to operate.

- 2 initiates the screen across from 1 to 5 by dribbling to the wing.

- Sequential passing reads are 2 or 2-to-5.

- 3 and 4 need to be ready to reposition themselves to become safety outlets.

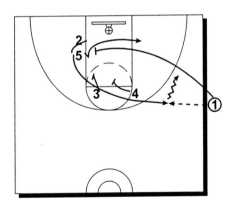

PLAY #97: SIDE OUT-OF-BOUNDS VERSUS A MAN-TO-MAN DEFENSE

Objective: A box set designed for a lob or to isolate a post player (5). One, two, or three passes for a shot.

Description: From a box set, 2 starts on the opposite block, 4 on the opposite elbow, 3 on the ballside block, and 5 at the ballside elbow. 2 starts the play by moving up to set a back screen for 5. 5 curls off of the back screen, looking for the lob from 1. If the lob is open, 1 throws it, but if it is not open, 2 steps out from the back screen and receives the inbound pass. As soon as 2 catches the ball, 4 sets a ball screen for him and 2 dribbles off the screen to the wing, looking to feed the ball to 5 at the low post. As 2 dribbles to the wing, 3 cuts hard to the ballside corner (Diagram 97a). If 5 was not open for the lob, his defender must have been in a denial position on top of him. If so, 5 seals him on the high side and gets the entry pass from 2 on the wing or 3 in the corner. If 5's defender moves in front of 5, then 2 can look to pass back to 4 for *the high-low entry (Diagram 97b)*.

Coaching Points:

• The lob may be available, but the primary function of this play is to isolate 5 in the low post and to be able to enter the ball to him no matter how he is being defended.

• 5 must work hard to seal his defender on whichever side the defender chooses, so the entry angle to the post is easy for 2 to read.

• The better the screen that 2 sets for 5, the more likely it is that both 5 and 2 will be open.

• Sequential passing reads are 1-to-5 on the lob, 1-to-2-to-5 at the low post, 1-to-2-to-3-to-5 baseline entry, and 1-to-2-to-4-to-5 high-low entry.

• 3 and 4 must be ready to reposition themselves to become safety outlets.

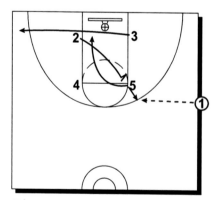

Diagram 97a

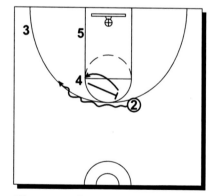

Diagram 97b

PLAY #98: SIDE OUT-OF-BOUNDS VERSUS A ZONE DEFENSE

Objective: Random set for a lob pass behind the zone. Three passes for a shot.

Description: From a random set, 2 starts at the foul line, 4 steps outside the opposite block, 3 at the opposite block, and 5 at the ballside block. 2 V-cuts and gets open at the top of the zone defense. After passing the ball to 2, 1 follows his pass and gets a return pass or handoff from 2. While that exchange is going on, 3 and 5 move behind the baseline of the zone and set screens on the backs of defenders X3 and X4. 1 receives the ball back from 2, takes a single dribble, and throws the lob to 4, who is cutting behind the zone and the screens set by 3 and 5.

Coaching Points:

- The lob pass must be made on the side of the basket where the screens are being set by 3 and 5 so that X5 is not involved in the play.

- The timing between 1, 2, and 4 needs to be perfect so that 4 is in the right place, ready to receive the lob after a single dribble by 1.

- 3 and 5 should not draw attention to themselves by cutting too fast. They have to make it look like they are just casually crossing under the zone. They need to set walking screens that get contact just before the lob pass is thrown.

- Sequential passing reads are 1-to-2-to-1-to-4.

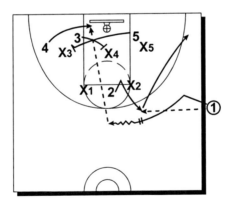

PLAY #99: SIDE OUT-OF-BOUNDS VERSUS A ZONE DEFENSE

Objective: Double-stack set designed for a short jumper in the side gap of the zone defense. One pass for a shot.

Description: From a double-stack set, 2 and 4 line up stacked on the opposite block and 3 and 5 start on the ballside block. 2 and 3 initiate the movement and spread the side of the zone with their cuts. 2 cuts quickly across the key to the ballside corner, dragging the baseline defender (X5) with him. 3 cuts up the inside of the key and to the top of the circle, dragging X2 with him. As soon as 2 and 3 begin their movement, 5 screens the middle defender on the baseline of the zone (X4) and 4 V-cuts to the basket behind X4, then cuts into the gap created by the cuts of 2 and 3. This setup should result in a catch, shoot, or catch-and-drive opportunity for 4.

Coaching Points:

- 1 can help 4 get open by ball faking to either 3 or 2 on their cuts.

- 5's screen is the key to 4 getting open. 5 must know where the middle defender is located and go find him to get contact.

- 4 steps behind the zone to disappear for a second before making a quick cut into the gap.

- Sequential passing reads are ball fake to 2 or 3, and then pass to 4.

- 2 and 3 need to be ready to reposition themselves to become safety outlets if 1 cannot pass to 4.

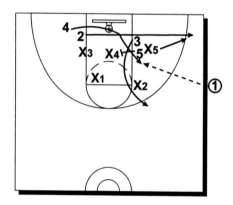

PLAY #100: SIDE OUT-OF-BOUNDS VERSUS A MAN-TO-MAN DEFENSE

Objective: Random set for a quick-and-easy, little-on-big ball screen and roll isolation for point guard and post player. One or two passes for a shot.

Description: From a random set, 2 starts at the opposite midpost area, 3 at the opposite elbow, 4 at the foul line, and 5 at the ballside low post. 2, 3, and 4 are just decoys in the play as 3 and 4 set a double staggered screen for 2 to cut back up to the top of the circle. After screening, 3 fades to the far opposite corner. 5 aligns himself directly between the ball and basket, and then pops out to the low wing or corner area to receive the inbound pass. As soon as 5 catches the ball, 1 follows his pass and sets a ball screen on the top of 5's defender. 5 uses the screen to drive over the top for a shot or a drop off to 1, who is rolling to the basket.

Coaching Points:

- This play is simple enough to be used at any level of play and can isolate any two offensive players you choose.

- If 3's defender comes to help as 5 drives off the ball screen and gets closer to the basket, then 5 has an outlet pass to 3 in the corner.

- Sequential passing reads are 1-to-5, 1-to-5-to-1 on the roll, and 1-to-5-to-3 in the corner.

- 2 and 4 need to be ready to reposition themselves to become safety outlets in case the ball cannot be inbounded to 5.

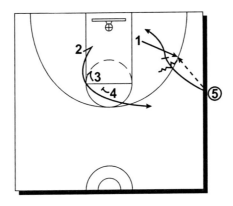

PLAY #101: SIDE OUT-OF-BOUNDS VERSUS A MAN-TO-MAN OR A ZONE DEFENSE

Objective: Random set designed to isolate your best shooter (2) and your best post (5) for quick options. One or two passes for a shot.

Description: From a random set, 3 starts at the opposite elbow, 4 at the ballside elbow, 2 outside 4 on the three-point line, and 5 at the ballside block. 4 starts with a screen for 2, who curls to the inside of the key and then circles back under 5 to the ballside corner. 1 looks for the lob to 2, and then reads the defense to see how 5 is being played at the low post. If 5's defender is behind him, 1 can throw a direct pass to 5. If 5's defender is on the high side, 1 passes to 2 in the corner for the entry pass. If 5's defender is in front of 5, then 1 passes to 4 stepping out off the screen for a high-low entry to 5. Against a zone, 3 fades to the opposite corner to occupy the far baseline defender and open up the low post for 5 to operate one-on-one.

Coaching Points:

- 2 cuts hard off the back screen by 4 and holds his hand up for the lob. The main focus of this play is isolating 5 in the low post, so unless it is wide open, the lob should not be thrown.

- 2's cut under 5 at the block should give 1 an indication of how 5's defender is going to be playing him, and where 1 should make his pass.

- 5 must seal his defender on whatever side he is being played to make the read easy for 1.

- If 2 has trouble making the entry pass to 5 at the low post, 5 can step out and set a ball screen for 2 in the corner.

- Sequential passing reads are 1-to-5, 1-to-2-to-5, and 1-to-4-to-5.

- 3 and 4 need to be ready to reposition themselves to become safety outlets.

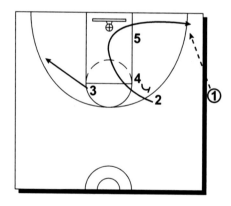

About the Author

Bruce Eamon Brown is a special presenter for the NAIA's "Champions of Character Program." Previously, he served as the athletic director at Northwest College in Kirkland, Washington. A retired coach, he worked at every level of education in his more than three decades of teaching and coaching. His coaching experiences included basketball, football, volleyball, and baseball at the junior high and high school levels, and basketball at the junior college and college levels. He was involved with championship teams at each level of competition.

Brown is a much sought-after speaker, who frequently addresses coaches, players, and parents on selected aspects concerning participation in sport. He has written several books, including the highly acclaimed *1001 Motivational Messages and Quotes: Teaching Character Through Sport* and *Another 1001 Motivational Messages and Quotes: Featuring the 7 Essentials of Great Teams*. He has also been the featured speaker on several well-received instructional videos:

- *Basketball Skills and Drills for Younger Players: Volume 7 – Individual Defense*
- *Basketball Skills and Drills for Younger Players: Volume 8 – Team Defense*
- *Basketball Skills and Drills for Younger Players: Volume 9 – Fast Break*
- *Basketball Skills and Drills for Younger Players: Volume 10 – Zone Offense*
- *Basketball Skills and Drills for Younger Players: Volume 11 – The Role of Parents in Athletics*
- *Fun Ways to End Basketball Practice*
- *Team Building Through Positive Conditioning*
- *Redefining the Term "Athlete" – Using the Five Core Values*
- *How to Teach Character Through Sport*

Brown and his wife, Dana, have five daughters, Allison, Katie, Shannon, Bridget, and Dana. The family resides in Camano Island, Washington.